Poison Ivy

This weed (above) causes an itchy
rash if you touch it. Poison ivy grows
as a vine or shrub. Try to remember
what the leaves look like, and do
not touch them or other parts of
the plant. If you do touch poison
ivy, washing your hands as soon as
possible may reduce the itching.
Your local drugstore will have
various remedies that will help.

World Book's

SCIENCE & NATURE GUIDES

AMPHIBIANS & REPTILES

OF THE UNITED STATES AND CANADA

World Book, Inc.
a Scott Fetzer company
Chicago

Scientific names

In this book, after the common name of an organism (life form) is given, that organism's scientific name usually appears. Scientific names are put into a special type of lettering, called italic, *which looks like this*.

The first name in a scientific name is the genus. A genus consists of very similar groups, but the members of these different groups usually cannot breed with one another. The second name given is the species. Every known organism belongs to a particular species. Members of the same species can breed with one another, and the young grow up to look very much like their parents.

An animal's scientific name is the same worldwide. This helps scientists and students to know which animal is being discussed, since the animal may have many different common names.

Therefore, when you see a name like *Agkistrodon contortrix,* you know that the genus is *Agkistrodon* and the species is *contortrix. Agkistrodon contortrix* is the scientific name for the northern copperhead (see page 22).

Snakebite first aid: page 40.

Countryside Code

1 **Always go exploring with a friend,** and always tell an adult where you are going.
2 **Do not touch animal nests or dens.**
3 **Keep clear of any wild animals that you find**—they may attack you if frightened.
4 **Keep to existing roads, trails, and pathways** wherever possible.
5 **Ask permission** before exploring or crossing private property.
6 **Leave fence gates as you find them.**
7 **Wear long pants, a hat, shoes, and a long-sleeved shirt** in tick country.

This edition published in the United States of America by World Book, Inc., Chicago.

WORLD BOOK and the GLOBE DEVICE are registered trademarks or trademarks of World Book, Inc.

World Book, Inc.
233 North Michigan Avenue
Chicago, IL 60601 USA

For information about other World Book publications, visit our Web site **http://www.worldbook.com,** or call **1-800-WORLDBK (967-5325).** For information about sales to schools and libraries, call **1-800-975-3250 (United States); 1-800-837-5365 (Canada).**

Copyright © 2005 Chrysalis Children's Book Group, an imprint of Chrysalis Books Group Plc
The Chrysalis Building, Bramley Road, London, W10 6SP
www.chrysalis.com

Library of Congress Cataloging-in-Publication Data

Amphibians & reptiles of the United States and Canada.
    p. cm. — (World Book's science & nature guides)
    Includes bibliographical references and index.
    ISBN 0-7166-4209-3 — ISBN 0-7166-4208-5 (set)
    1. Amphibians—North America—Juvenile literature. 2. Reptiles—North America—Juvenile literature. 3. Amphibians—North America—Identification—Juvenile literature. 4. Reptiles—North America—Identification—Juvenile literature. I. Title: Amphibians and reptiles of the United States and Canada. II. World Book, Inc. III. Series.

QL651.A552 2005
597.9'097—dc22
                                        2004043487

Habitat paintings by Alan Male; headbands by Antonia Phillips; identification and activities illustrations by Mr. Gay Galsworthy.

For World Book:
General Managing Editor: Paul A. Kobasa
Editorial: Shawn Brennan, Maureen Liebenson, Christine Sullivan
Research: Madolynn Cronk, Lynn Durbin, Cheryl Graham, Karen McCormack, Loranne Shields, Hilary Zawidowski
Librarian: Jon Fjortoft
Permissions: Janet Peterson
Graphics and Design: Sandra Dyrlund, Anne Fritzinger
Indexing: Aamir Burki, David Pofelski
Pre-press and Manufacturing: Carma Fazio, Steve Hueppchen, Jared Svoboda, Madelyn Underwood
Text Processing: Curley Hunter, Gwendolyn Johnson
Proofreading: Anne Dillon

Printed in China
1 2 3 4 5 6 7 8 9 10 09 08 07 06 05 04

Contents

Entries **like this**
indicate pages
featuring
projects you
can do!

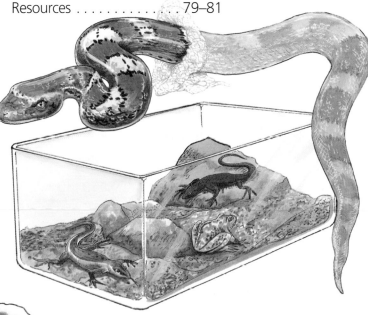

Introduction To Amphibians & Reptiles

Amphibians and reptiles have lived on Earth for hundreds of millions of years; today there are about 4,000 species (kinds) of amphibians and 6,500 species of reptiles. Many species have become extinct (have died out) since the first amphibian crawled out of the sea about 360 million years ago. Reptiles appeared about 35 million years later but became the dominant animal group only about 248 million years ago. The dinosaurs were reptiles.

This book shows you where and how to look for these animals and what you can expect to see in different habitats. You will discover what makes an amphibian different from a reptile, what these animals like to eat, and how many young they have. The scientific study of amphibians and reptiles is called herpetology. One day, if you become an expert on these animals, you will be a herpetologist.

An amphibian's life cycle

Most amphibians breed in or near water. Some female amphibians lay a mass of eggs in water, others lay one egg at a time, which is attached to a water plant. The eggs hatch after a few hours, days, or weeks.

The young hatchlings are called larvae. They take from a few days to several months to develop into adults and climb onto land. Animals that change form before becoming adults undergo a process called metamorphosis.

Some kinds of amphibians never change into an adult form, but stay in a larval form and live in water their entire life. Some amphibians move to land, and some of these, such as lungless salamanders, never develop lungs and instead breathe through their moist skin.

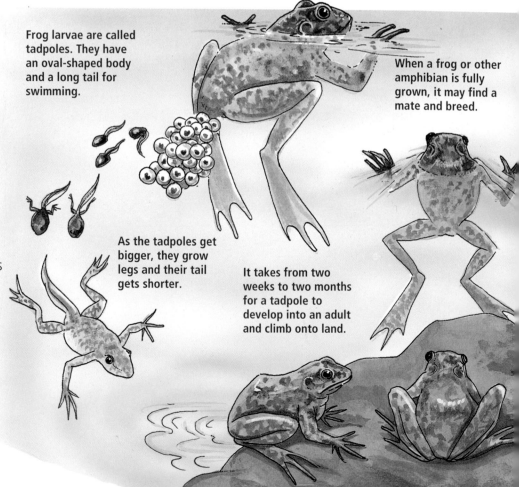

Frogs breed in or near water. The males call to attract the females. The females lay their eggs in water.

Frog larvae are called tadpoles. They have an oval-shaped body and a long tail for swimming.

When a frog or other amphibian is fully grown, it may find a mate and breed.

As the tadpoles get bigger, they grow legs and their tail gets shorter.

It takes from two weeks to two months for a tadpole to develop into an adult and climb onto land.

How to use this book

To identify an animal that you do not recognize—for example, the salamander or lizard shown on the top half of this page—follow these steps.

1 **Note the animal's size, shape, and color** in your field notebook (see page 14). Do a quick sketch, if possible.

2 **See if the animal has any special feaures,** such as spiky scales, claws, or webbed toes (pages 6–7 show you what to look for to tell an amphibian from a reptile).

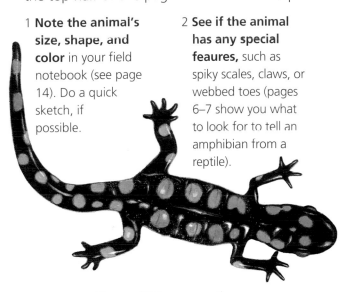

3 **Decide which habitat you are in.** The descriptions at the beginning of each section will help you. Each habitat has a different picture band (see below on this page).

4 **Look through the pages that cover your habitat.** The picture and information with each animal will help you to identify it. This spotted salamander (left) is an amphibian that belongs to the mole salamander family (see page 21).

5 **If you cannot find the animal there,** look through the other sections. This collared lizard (see above and page 58) is a reptile that belongs to the Iguanid family.

6 **If you cannot find the animal in this book,** it may be very rare. Try looking in other books about amphibians and reptiles.

A reptile's life cycle

Some reptiles lay eggs, and others give birth to miniature versions of themselves. Many egg-laying reptiles lay their eggs in a hole dug in the sand or under a rock or leaves, then leave them. Among some kinds of lizards and snakes, the female keeps her eggs within her body until they hatch. Still other kinds of female lizards and snakes do not form eggs at all, but give birth to fully formed young.

Top-of-page picture bands

This book is divided into different sections. Each section has a different picture band at the top of the page. These are shown below.

Backyards & Parks

Forests & Woodlands

Streams & Rivers

Lakes, Ponds, & Marshes

Grasslands

Deserts & Arid Scrub

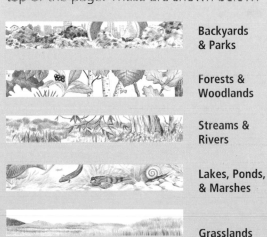

Reptile or Amphibian?

When you are trying to identify a reptile or an amphibian, look at the animal's shape, skin texture, feet, and color.
- Is the skin scaly or smooth?
- Do the feet have claws or webbing?

It is easy to recognize snakes, which are reptiles, and so their traits are not discussed on these identification pages. But it is quite easy to confuse an amphibian—such as a salamander—with a reptile like a lizard. Once you know which clues to look for, however, you will soon be able to spot the differences between the two groups.

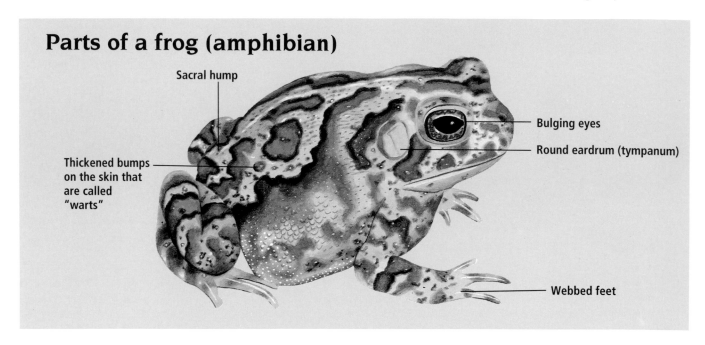

Parts of a frog (amphibian)

Sacral hump

Bulging eyes

Round eardrum (tympanum)

Thickened bumps on the skin that are called "warts"

Webbed feet

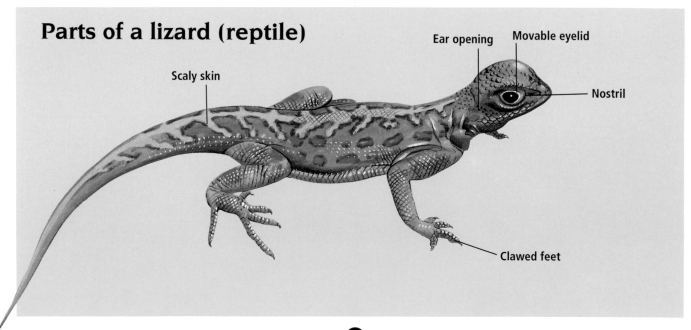

Parts of a lizard (reptile)

Ear opening

Movable eyelid

Scaly skin

Nostril

Clawed feet

Skin, scales, and shells

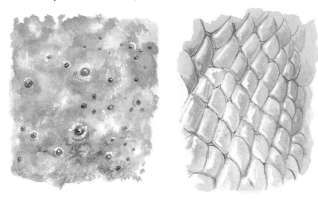

Amphibian   **Reptile**

Amphibians have moist, flexible skin without scales. Sometimes their skin is smooth and sometimes rough, but it is never scaly. Reptiles always have tough, dry, scaly skin, and sometimes the scales are spiky too. Such reptiles as tortoises, turtles, and terrapins also have a hard shell that protects their body.

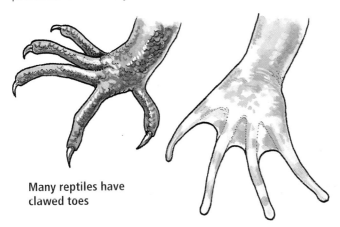

Many reptiles have clawed toes

Feet and toes

Many amphibians have webbed feet

Many reptiles have clawed toes, but amphibians never have claws. Many amphibians have webbed toes. Both true frogs and tree frogs have webbing, but toads do not.

Safety first

When you go searching for amphibians or reptiles in the wild, be very cautious. **Don't touch or pick up animals you find,** because some animals bite. See page 40 for what to do if you are bitten by a snake.

Many amphibians and reptiles, including poisonous snakes, like to hide under rocks, dead leaves, and rotten logs. If disturbed, they will try to escape as quickly as possible, but they may try to attack you first. **So, don't take risks. Never move rocks or logs with your bare hands.** It is much safer to use a stick or a boot to gently move logs, leaves, or rocks aside. Wear boots or sneakers and long pants for your expeditions (see page 14).

Body shape and color

The color and pattern of amphibians and reptiles often vary, depending on the age of the animal. Sometimes adults are a completely different color from the young. Frogs are usually slim-bodied, while toads are more squat in shape. Both toads and frogs are tailless, but most lizards have tails, sometimes longer than the body. Even snakes have tails, though it is hard to tell where the tail begins, because snakes have no legs.

Toad

Tree frog

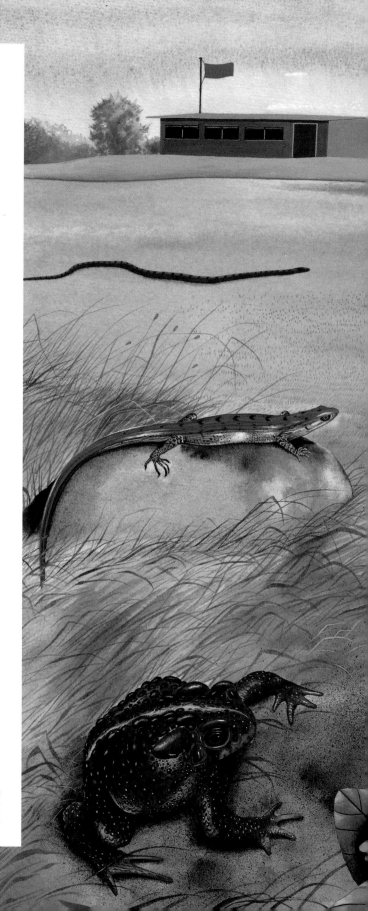

Backyards & Parks

The variety of animals that you are likely to see in your backyard depends on the area around your house, since reptiles and amphibians usually visit from surrounding areas of meadow, woodland, and other habitats. The most common backyard visitors are those that prefer a mixed habitat.

Backyard reptiles and amphibians have to tolerate people constantly disturbing their habitat—by gardening, for example. Frogs, toads, lungless salamanders, and some small snakes are the most familiar backyard inhabitants. They usually live under rocks, logs, among garden shrubs, or around garbage and compost heaps. Frogs living in built-up areas may depend on an ornamental garden pond for breeding.

If you want to encourage these animals into your backyard, try to leave an area to grow wild. You may be lucky enough to attract box turtles and hognose snakes if you have an undisturbed corner in your garden. Trees, shrubs, sheds, and walls provide good hiding places and hunting grounds for lizards, frogs, and some small snakes, too. Some common backyard reptiles, including brown snakes, hide so well that, unless you are very observant, you may never even know they share your backyard.

This picture shows reptiles and amphibians from this section—how many do you recognize?

Clockwise from the top left: northern brown snake, American toad, southern alligator lizard, and the common garter snake in the center.

Fowler's Toad
(Bufo woodhousii fowleri)

Fowler's toad is usually gray, greenish, or brown, with blotches on its back. It looks similar to the American toad, but it has more warts on the largest of its dark spots, and there are no spots on its belly. You are most likely to see this toad in the evening when it is searching for insects. During the day, it usually stays in its burrow. Fowler's toads live in backyards and wooded areas with sandy soil.

Animal group: Amphibian
Family: True toad
Size: 2–3 in (5–7.5 cm)
Eats insects and other small invertebrates

American Toad
(Bufo americanus)

This big, knobbly toad favors damp areas in which to live. The American toad is usually brown, dull red, or olive with a spotted belly. It has big, bony crests above each eye and sometimes a light stripe down the middle of its back. It is covered with orange or brown lumps, which are known as "warts." Warts on a toad are not bumps caused by a virus, as they would be in humans. They are just thickened areas of skin on a toad, and you cannot get warts from these bumps. **Many amphibians do secrete poisonous chemicals,** however. See page 15 about catching and handling both reptiles and amphibians.

Animal group: Amphibian
Family: True toad
Size: 2–4 in (5–10 cm)
Eats insects and other small invertebrates

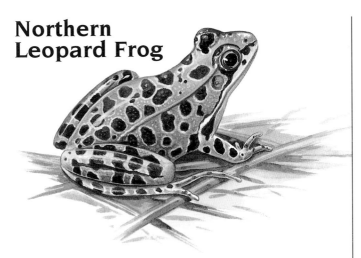

Northern Leopard Frog

(Rana pipiens)
This slim-bodied frog may be either green or brown. You can easily recognize it by its round, dark, leopardlike spots with light edges. The species likes wet, grassy fields, meadows, and marshes. They hop in a zig-zag pattern. The leopard frog's call sounds like a long, rattling snore.
Animal group: Amphibian
Family: True frog
Size: 2–5 in (5–12.5 cm)
Eats insects and other small invertebrates

Squirrel Tree Frog
(Hyla squirella)

This frog changes color from green to brown to blend in with its surroundings. It sometimes has spots or yellow marks on its back. It may also have a dark mark between its eyes. Squirrel tree frogs like all kinds of habitats, as long as they are wet. You can often hear their ducklike calls after summer rain showers. These frogs are very busy at night, and often come near houses to catch moths and other insects. During the day, they prefer to hide among garden shrubs, sometimes in large groups.
Animal group: Amphibian
Family: Tree frog
Size: 1–1¾ in (2.5–4.5 cm)
Eats insects

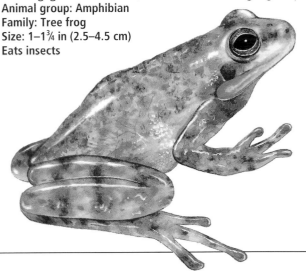

Woodhouse's Toad
(Bufo woodhoussii)

This toad lives in many habitats including backyards, desert streams, marshes, and even rain puddles. You are most likely to see one at night, when it is out catching insects. It is usually yellow, green, or brown, with a light stripe on its back and dark warts on its skin. There are two bony crests above its eyes. Listen for this toad's call, which sounds like a sheep bleating.
Animal group: Amphibian
Family: True toad
Size: 2–4 in (5–10 cm)
Eats insects and other small invertebrates

Eastern Hognose Snake
(Heterodon platyrhinos)

This plump snake is named after its piglike snout. It can be various colors from yellow to brown to gray, and it is usually spotted. The eastern hognose snake has a curious way of defending itself, which has earned it such nicknames as "puff adder" and "blow viper." If it is disturbed, the snake puffs out its body, spreads its neck, hisses, then strikes at the intruder. This makes the snake look bigger than it really is, so it seems more threatening. If this performance does not work, the snake turns over and lays very still, pretending to be dead. In summer, the female lays from about 5 to 60 eggs in a shallow hole.

Animal group: Reptile
Family: Colubrid snake—Size: 20–45 in (51–115 cm)
Eats frogs and toads, and also crickets and other insects

Common Garter Snake

(Thamnophis sirtalis)
You can find these snakes in parks, meadows, woodlands, and yards. They usually live close to ponds, streams, and marshes, where there is plenty of moisture. Garter snakes are most active when they search for food during the day. Common garter snakes may be many shades of green, yellow, or gray, but they nearly always have three yellowish stripes along their back and sides. These snakes mate in spring, and the females give birth to an average of 18 young in late summer to fall.
Animal group: Reptile
Family: Colubrid snake
Size: 20–30 in (51–76 cm)
Eats frogs, toads, salamanders, earthworms, and sometimes mice and small fish

Southern Alligator Lizard

Animal group: Reptile—Family: Anguid lizard—Size: 10–17 in (25.5–42.5 cm)—Eats chiefly insects, spiders, and scorpions

(Elgaria multicarinata)
This long, shiny lizard has short legs and moves very stiffly because its hard scales act like a suit of armor. Its color varies from reddish-brown to yellowish-gray. The irises of its eyes are yellow, and it has dark bands on its back and tail. Look on bushes in open forests where there are oak trees, and you may see one of these lizards using its tail to cling to twigs and branches as it climbs. The female lays an average of 12 eggs during the warmest months of the year.

Eastern Box Turtle
(Terrapene carolina)

This pretty turtle has a hinged lower shell that shuts snugly against the upper shell when the turtle needs to hide. Eastern box turtles are usually brown, patterned with orange or yellow blotches. The males have red eyes and the females have yellow-brown eyes. These turtles like wet meadows, forests, and fields. Look for them in the early morning or after a summer shower, when they come out to search for their favorite foods—slugs and strawberries. Some of these turtles live for more than a hundred years. They are land turtles, but they sometimes like to soak in mud or water. In hot, dry weather, they burrow under a log for shelter. The female lays eggs in a hole that she digs in the soil.

Animal group: Reptile
Family: Pond and marsh turtles
Shell size: 4–8 in (10–20 cm)
Eats a variety of animals, plants, and mushrooms

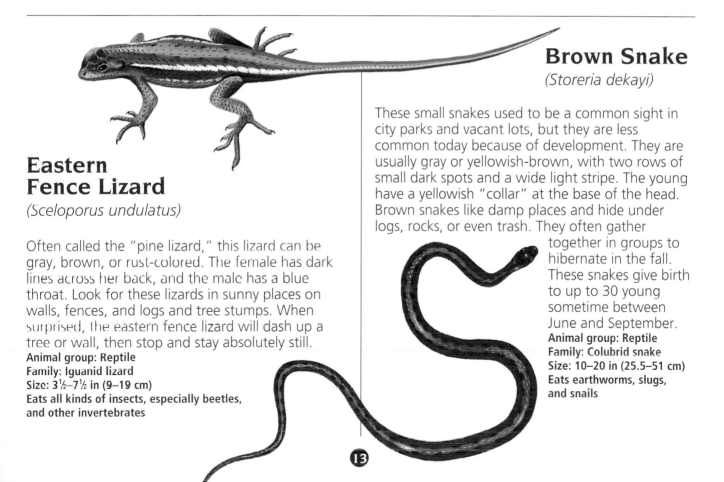

Eastern Fence Lizard
(Sceloporus undulatus)

Often called the "pine lizard," this lizard can be gray, brown, or rust-colored. The female has dark lines across her back, and the male has a blue throat. Look for these lizards in sunny places on walls, fences, and logs and tree stumps. When surprised, the eastern fence lizard will dash up a tree or wall, then stop and stay absolutely still.
Animal group: Reptile
Family: Iguanid lizard
Size: 3½–7½ in (9–19 cm)
Eats all kinds of insects, especially beetles, and other invertebrates

Brown Snake
(Storeria dekayi)

These small snakes used to be a common sight in city parks and vacant lots, but they are less common today because of development. They are usually gray or yellowish-brown, with two rows of small dark spots and a wide light stripe. The young have a yellowish "collar" at the base of the head. Brown snakes like damp places and hide under logs, rocks, or even trash. They often gather together in groups to hibernate in the fall. These snakes give birth to up to 30 young sometime between June and September.
Animal group: Reptile
Family: Colubrid snake
Size: 10–20 in (25.5–51 cm)
Eats earthworms, slugs, and snails

Looking For Species

Most reptiles and amphibians are afraid of people and so they try to conceal themselves from our view. To be successful in finding and watching them, you will need plenty of patience. As with bird watching, you will improve greatly with practice. When you first go out searching, you may not find anything, but you will begin to see animals once you learn where to look.

A good way to start is to join a local wildlife group or visit a zoo near you to find out which species are common in your area. Never go alone on any animal-spotting expedition, always take a friend.

Equipment

You do not need any special equipment to observe animals. Sharp eyes, however, are really helpful! A pair of binoculars and a camera are also useful. Take a field notebook, like the one shown above, and pens and pencils to make notes. Wear sturdy shoes or boots if you are walking through brush or undergrowth where there may be snakes. Wear long pants, a long-sleeved shirt, and a hat if you are in tick country.

Keeping records

Making notes in a field notebook is an excellent way to learn from your observations. Your notes and photos will help you identify the animals.

1 **Give a name to each new site that you visit.** Write down the date and what sort of habitat it is (pond, garden, field, etc.).
2 **Each time you visit that site, record what the weather is like** and what time of day it is.
3 **When you find a reptile or amphibian, watch it carefully.** Make a note of its shape, color, and size to help in identification.
4 **Take a photograph if you can!** If you approach quietly, many species will stay still.
5 **Write down what the animal is doing (sleeping, eating, etc.),** and what noise it is making.

Catching & handling reptiles & amphibians

DO NOT APPROACH OR TRY TO CATCH ANY SNAKE unless told by an adult expert that it is safe to do so. Only 20 of the 100 some species in North America are poisonous, but these few venomous snakes are very dangerous. See page 40 for what to do if you are bitten by a snake. If you can, visit a children's zoo where you can learn to safely handle a snake.

Although most lizards and turtles are harmless, they are best observed from a distance. Large lizards and some turtles can give you a nasty bite. In the United States, there is only one species of poisonous lizard, the large Gila monster. No poisonous lizards live in Canada.

You may be able to catch newts, young salamanders, frogs, or toads using a dip net in a pond. Most salamanders, newts, and frogs can be safely handled. You should handle these amphibians, however, only if a teacher or adult expert with you is certain that the species is not endangered and that the water is clean and safe. Always wash your hands after handling any animals.

Amphibians secrete an unpleasant liquid from their skins. This can cause swelling and discomfort if it enters a cut or gets in your mouth or eyes. Rinse the cut, or your eyes or mouth, thoroughly with clean water if this happens.

Adopt a site

If you have a favorite pond, wood, or field near you, visit it regularly (perhaps once a month) and get to know it really well. Keep track of:

- **Which animals live there,** and which are just passing through.
- **What happens there in winter and in spring.** Make a plan of the site, name the different areas, and mark on the plan where the animals are found. You could repeat this four times a year.

Forests & Woodlands

Damp, shady forests and woodlands make an ideal habitat for amphibians that need to keep their skin cool and moist, such as salamanders and frogs. The main types of forest in the United States and Canada are evergreen and deciduous. An evergreen forest may contain pine, fir, and spruce trees. All these trees have needlelike leaves and are coniferous—that is, the trees produce cones. In these forests, summers are usually hot and winters cold and snowy.

In the deciduous forests of the United States and Canada, there are oak, maple, beech, and elm trees, among others. These trees form a thick canopy of leaves in summer; they then lose their leaves in winter, forming a dense layer of leaf litter on the forest floor. This litter provides a good hiding place for salamanders and newts. There are many other places to shelter in a forest, such as under a pile of logs, inside a rotten tree stump, under the bark of a tree, or high up in the trees.

Many forest reptiles are good tree climbers, and black rat snakes, corn snakes, and rubber boas often climb trees in search of food. Some reptiles are well camouflaged to blend in with the bark or leaves of the trees.

This picture shows reptiles and amphibians from this section—how many do you recognize?

Clockwise from top left: broadhead skink, corn snake, ringneck snake, redback salamander, spotted salamander, and a wood frog.

Blanchard's Cricket Frog
(Acris crepitans blanchardi)

This tiny frog belongs to the tree frog family, but it doesn't like to climb trees. It prefers to stay on the ground and likes sunny, wet, overgrown meadows where it can live close to a slow-moving stream or shallow pool. Its rough skin is usually light brown or gray, and it always has a dark triangle shape between its eyes and a ragged dark stripe on its long hind legs. Its call sounds like a clicking noise.

Animal group: Amphibian
Family: Tree frog
Size: ½–1½ in (1–4 cm)
Eats insects and other small invertebrates

Pacific Tree Frog
(Hyla regilla)

The high-pitched, musical call of this frog is a familiar sound. It lives mainly in forests and woodlands where there are ponds, ditches, and streams—but it can adapt to many environments. This is a rough-skinned frog that can change in color very rapidly from green to dark brown or black, often with dark spots. There is usually a dark stripe running across each eye. Pacific tree frogs breed from January to early summer and lay their eggs in quiet streams and ponds.

Animal group: Amphibian—Family: Tree frog
Size: 1–2 in (2.5–5 cm)
Eats insects and other small invertebrates

Wood Frog
(Rana sylvatica)

The wood frog is pink, green, tan, or dark brown with a dark patch like a mask over its face. These frogs like damp woodland areas. This is the only kind of frog that exists north of the Arctic Circle. Wood frogs breed in early spring and lay masses of eggs in ponds; they attach the eggs to underwater plants. Wood frogs are usually out during the day. In the winter months they hibernate in leaf litter on the woodland floor.

Animal group: Amphibian
Family: True frog
Size: 1½–3¼ in (4–8 cm)
Eats insects and other small invertebrates

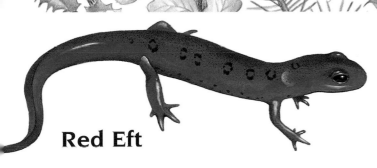

Red Eft

Animal group: Amphibian—**Family:** Newt
Size: ½–3½ in (1–9 cm)
Eats invertebrates
WARNING: These newts have a poisonous substance in their skin that makes them taste nasty to predators. It is not dangerous to humans, but if you touch an eft, wash your hands.

(Notophthalmus viridescens viridescens)
Red efts are the brightly colored young of red-spotted newts (see page 48), and they live on land rather than in water. You can see the efts in damp woodlands after a shower of rain as they search for their favorite food, small invertebrates. They are red or orange to reddish-brown with orange-red spots on their back. After one to three years, the efts mature into adult newts and take to the water in ponds, lakes, and quiet streams. They breed from late winter to early spring, laying 200 to 400 eggs, 1 at a time, on water plants. The young larvae hatch about three to five weeks later and change into efts in late summer or early fall.

Roughskin Newt
(Taricha granulosa)

You can tell this newt apart from others by its very warty skin. It is usually light brown, green, or black on top, with an orange or yellow belly. If threatened, this newt shows off its colorful belly as a warning signal. Roughskin newts live under logs, rocks, and bark in forests. They breed from December to July and from October to November. The female lays her eggs one at a time on water plants, and the young hatch 5 to 10 weeks later. They change into adults when they are 2 to 3 inches (5 to 7.5 centimeters) long.

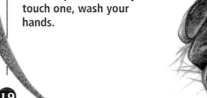

Animal group: Amphibian
Family: Newt
Size: 5–8 in (12.5–20 cm)
Eats insects, slugs, worms, and other small invertebrates
WARNING: This newt produces a substance in its skin that is poisonous to humans. Do not touch it.

Eastern Spadefoot
(Scaphiopus holbrookii)

This is the only spadefoot toad to be found east of the Mississippi River, and you can recognize it by its low, grunting call. A group of these toads makes such a noise that you can hear them up to half a mile (0.8 kilometer) away. Most eastern spadefoots are olive or brown with red spots, and they usually have two yellowish lines running along the back. Like other spadefoot toads, they are good at digging, and they burrow in the soil for shelter. Their burrows keep them safe from predators and from drought. These toads breed year-round in the South and from early spring to early fall in the North, usually at night following heavy rains. They lay their eggs on pond plants. The tadpoles hatch after two days and change into adults in two to eight weeks.

Animal group: Amphibian—**Family:** Spadefoot toad
Size: 1¾–3¼ in (4.5–8 cm)
Eats insects and other small invertebrates
WARNING: Some people are allergic to the substance produced in the skin of spadefoots. If you touch one, wash your hands.

Northern Slimy Salamander
(Plethodon glutinosus)

This large, shiny, black salamander is speckled with many small gray or golden spots on its head, back, and tail. It is named after the sticky substance its skin produces to put off predators. Slimy salamanders breed in spring and fall in the North, and in summer in the South. They lay a clutch of 6 to 36 eggs in a rotten log or underground, and the female guards the nest until the larvae hatch.

Animal group: Amphibian
Family: Lungless salamander
Size: 4½–8 in (11.5–20 cm)
Hunts at night for small invertebrates on the forest floor

Sierra Nevada Ensatina
(Ensatina eschscholtzii platensis)

You can recognize this salamander because its tail is narrow instead of thick at the base. If a predator grabs an ensatina by its tail, the tail breaks off so the ensatina can escape. The tail then regrows a few weeks later—a trick many salamanders use. When threatened, these salamanders arch their tail. The male's tail is often longer than its body. Ensatinas can be all sorts of colors from reddish-brown to dark brown, with cream, yellow, or orange spots or blotches. They live in redwood forests, and also pine, cedar, and maple forests. In cold or dry weather, they shelter in animal burrows and among rotten logs and roots. They mate in late spring to early summer, and the female lays 7 to 25 eggs underground and cares for them until they hatch in fall or early winter. These salamanders may live for up to 15 years in the wild.
Animal group: Amphibian
Family: Lungless salamander
Size: 3–5½ in (7.5–14 cm)
Eats spiders, beetles, crickets, and springtails

Redback Salamander

(Plethodon cinereus)
This long, slim salamander usually has a wide red, orange, or pink stripe along its back from head to tail, and its belly is mottled black and white. You are most likely to spot one in forests, although they are found in many habitats, even vacant city lots. They like cool, damp coniferous or mixed forest, where they hide during the day under leaves or stones. They are able to tolerate very cold weather, so they survive in the extreme northeast of the United States and in Canada. These salamanders may mate in fall or the following spring, but the female waits until summer to lay her 6 to 12 eggs under a stone or inside a rotten log. She curls her body around the eggs and watches over them until they hatch some two months later.
Animal group: Amphibian
Family: Lungless salamander
Size: 2½–5 in (6.5–12.5 cm)
Hunts at night for small insects, slugs, and worms

Spotted Salamander
(Ambystoma maculatum)

This pretty salamander spends most of its life hiding underground, so you will be very lucky to see one in the wild. It is heavily built, with two rows of yellow or orange spots along its body from head to tail. Spotted salamanders live in eastern hardwood forests close to water. They breed in spring in the North and even earlier in the South. The female lays one or more masses of eggs, which hatch into larvae in one to two months, and become adults in two to four months. These salamanders can live for up to 20 years.

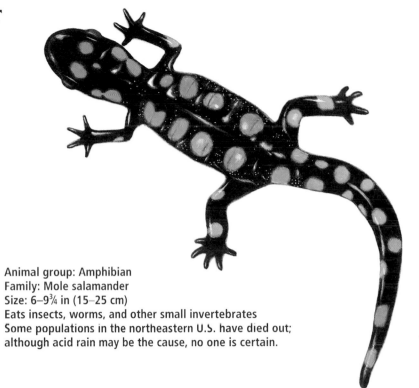

Animal group: Amphibian
Family: Mole salamander
Size: 6–9¾ in (15–25 cm)
Eats insects, worms, and other small invertebrates
Some populations in the northeastern U.S. have died out; although acid rain may be the cause, no one is certain.

Blotched Tiger Salamander
(Ambystoma tigrinum melanostictum)

All species of tiger salamander are the largest land salamanders in the world. They have a plump body, a wide head, and small eyes. These salamanders are often out at night after a heavy rain, hunting for food. They can be found in forests, wet meadows, and along streams. They breed in late winter in the Southern States and in spring and summer in the North, laying their eggs in temporary pools and streams. The eggs hatch into larvae that turn into adults when they are about 4 inches (10 centimeters) long.

Animal group: Amphibian
Family: Mole salamander
Size: 6–13 in (15–33 cm)
Eats earthworms, insects, small fish, and other amphibians

Forests & Woodlands

Northern Copperhead

(Agkistrodon contortrix)
The copperhead is plump, with reddish-brown bands across its body, but not on its head. The snake can be copper, orange, or even pinkish in color. These snakes like wooded hillsides above streams where they shelter under rotten logs and large, flat stones. During the day in spring and fall, they bask in the sun, and in the warm summer months they come out at night. They mate and give birth to 2 to 14 live young in late summer or early fall. The young have yellow-tipped tails, which they twitch to attract unsuspecting prey.

Animal group: Reptile
Family: Pit viper
Size: 30–48 in (76.2–122 cm)
Eats small mice, frogs, lizards, and caterpillars
WARNING: This snake is poisonous and should not be approached!

Northern Black Racer

(Coluber constrictor constrictor)

Animal group: Reptile
Family: Colubrid snake
Size: 42–72 in (106.6–183 cm)
Eats large insects, frogs, lizards, other snakes, rodents, and birds

This slender snake has a shiny black back and a lighter belly. It is alert and fast-moving and speeds away very quickly when chased. It can slither up trees to escape from a predator or eat birds' eggs. When it is cornered, it fights ferociously. Northern black racers mate in spring, and the females lay 5 to 25 eggs under a rotten log or rocks, or in a mammal's burrow. Sometimes several females lay their eggs in the same place. The young hatch sometime between July and September.

Rubber Boa
(Charina bottae)

This olive-green or brown snake looks like a toy snake made of rubber. It is all one color, with large scales on the top of its head and small eyes. It has a short, wide snout and a short blunt tail, so it is difficult to tell which end is which. Rubber boas live in coniferous forests and damp woodlands, where they shelter under rotten logs and in leaf litter. These snakes are good at swimming, burrowing, and climbing, and they use their tail to hold on to branches as they climb. Rubber boas mate in spring and the female gives birth to live young sometime between August and September.

Animal group: Reptile
Family: Boa and python
Size: 14–33 in (35–84 cm)
This snake is a constrictor and hunts at night for birds, lizards, and small mammals

California Slender Salamander
(Batrachoseps attenuatus)

This long-bodied, long-tailed salamander has very short legs and small feet, which makes it easy to recognize. It is usually blackish on top, with a pink, red, or brown band on its back. These salamanders live on the coast and in the central valley of California, especially in redwood forests, where they shelter under logs, bark, and damp leaf litter. They mate in late fall and winter, and the females lay a clutch of 4 to 21 eggs under rocks or logs. Often, several females use the same nest.

Animal group: Amphibian
Family: Lungless salamander
Size: 3–5½ in (7.5–14 cm)
Eats small invertebrates

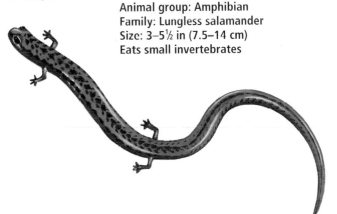

Arboreal Salamander

(Aneides lugubris)
This yellow-spotted salamander is an excellent tree climber. Look for it on rainy days in oak woodlands. During the dry summer months, it hides in tree holes and rodent burrows. When it rains, this salamander comes out to hunt for insects in the trees and in leaf litter on the woodland floor. Arboreal salamanders breed in late spring and early summer, the female then lays 12 to 24 eggs in a rotten log, a tree hollow, or a hole in the ground. The female tends the eggs until they hatch three to four months later.

Animal group: Amphibian
Family: Lungless salamander
Size: 4½–7¼ in (11.5–18.5 cm)
Feeds on insects and other small invertebrates

Eastern Diamondback Rattlesnake
(*Crotalus adamanteus*)

The eastern diamondback is the largest and most dangerous rattlesnake in the United States. Its bite is so deadly that it can easily kill a human so, if you see one, **keep well away.**
Rattlesnakes usually rattle their tails to warn away intruders, but not always. This snake has a pattern of dark diamonds with light centers on its back. There are also light diagonal lines on each side of its head. These rattlesnakes live in dry oak and pine forests of the south, sheltering during the day in burrows, beneath stumps and logs, or in thickets of palmetto. The female gives birth to 7 to 21 young sometime between July and October, each snakelet measures about 12 inches (30 centimeters) long.
Animal group: Reptile—Family: Pit viper
Size: 36–96 in (90–240 cm)
Feeds on rodents, rabbit-sized mammals, and birds
WARNING: Avoid this snake; its bite is deadly!

Timber Rattlesnake
(*Crotalus horridus*)

This rattlesnake is named for the hardwood forests where it lives. It is sometimes called the "velvet-tailed rattler" or "banded rattler." It may be yellowish with dark crossbars and a black tail, or almost all black. It comes out during the day from April to October, and it hunts on warm summer evenings, as well. In northern areas, these snakes gather in large numbers in the fall to hibernate in rocky dens with copperheads and rat snakes. Timber rattlesnakes can live for up to 30 years or more in the wild. They mate in early spring or fall, and the female gives birth to up to a dozen young.
Animal group: Reptile—Family: Pit viper
Size: 35–75 in (89–190 cm)
Eats rats and mice
WARNING: While not as deadly as the eastern diamondback, this snake is dangerously poisonous. Avoid this snake!

Black Rat Snake
(*Elaphe obsoleta obsoleta*)

This big, black snake is a powerful constrictor. It is an excellent climber and sometimes makes its home in a hole high up in a tree. These snakes look similar to western coachwhips (see page 60) and northern black racers (see page 22), but rat snakes have rougher scales. The black rat snake is found in hardwood forests. It mates and, sometime between June and August, the female lays a clutch of 5 to 30 eggs in a rotten log, leaf litter, or under a rock. The young hatch several weeks later. These snakes hibernate in winter and often share their den with timber rattlesnakes and copperheads.

Animal group: Reptile
Family: Colubrid snake
Size: 42–72 in (107–183 cm)
Eats birds and their eggs, mice, lizards, and small mammals

Corn Snake

(Elaphe guttata guttata)

This long, beautiful snake is orange or yellow with large blotches along its back. There is a dark mark shaped like a spearpoint on the top of its head. This snake's name probably comes from the checkered pattern on its belly, which is similar to the pattern on Indian corn. This snake is also called the "red rat snake." The corn snake is active mainly at night, but you may see it in the early evening. It likes wooded groves and rocky hillsides, and it climbs trees in search of prey. Corn snakes mate from March to May, and the female lays a clutch of 3 to 21 eggs from May to July. The young hatch sometime between July and September.

Animal group: Reptile—Family: Colubrid snake
Size: 30–48 in (76.5–122 cm)—Eats rats, mice, birds, and bats

Ringneck Snake

(Diadophis punctatus)

You cannot mistake this small, slim snake—it has a distinct yellow, orange, or cream ring around its neck. Its back is gray, olive, brown, or black, and it has a bright yellow, red, or orange belly. Ringneck snakes like to hide under flat rocks, logs, and loose tree bark. They are found in moist forests and rocky, wooded hillsides. They mate in the spring or fall, and the females lay clutches of 1 to 10 white or yellowish eggs in a nesting site. After about eight weeks, the young hatch. When ringneck snakes are threatened, they twist their tail to show their colorful underside. This has given them the nickname of "corkscrew snakes."

Animal group: Reptile
Family: Colubrid snake
Size: 10–30 in (25.5–76.5 cm)
Eats insects, small salamanders, earthworms, small lizards, and snakes

Forests & Woodlands

Eastern Coral Snake

(*Micrurus fulvius*)
It is very important to learn the difference between this **poisonous** snake and the harmless scarlet kingsnake (see page 27) that mimics it. The poisonous coral snake has wide red and black rings separated by a narrow yellow ring. Its head is completely black. Coral snakes like moist areas near water in hardwood or pine forests. They often shelter under decaying tree trunks or leaves. The female lays from 3 to 12 eggs in June and the young hatch in September.
Animal group: Reptile—Family: Coral snake
Size: 20–40 in (51–100 cm)
Eats lizards and other (smaller) snakes
WARNING: This snake's deadly bite can kill you. Remember, the "red-yellow-black" coloring means danger!

Redbelly Snake

(*Storeria occipitomaculata*)

This small snake is brown, gray, or black, usually with a plain red belly. It always has three light spots at the base of its neck. The redbelly snake likes wooded hills or mountains and is quite widespread over the central and eastern United States. These snakes mate in spring or fall and the female gives birth to between 1 and 21 young. If alarmed, the redbelly snake pulls its upper lip back.

Animal group: Reptile
Family: Colubrid snake
Size: 8–16 in (20–40 cm)
Feeds on insects,
earthworms, and slugs

Eastern Kingsnake

Animal group: Reptile—Family: Colubrid snake—Size: 18–72 in (46–180 cm)—Eats snakes, including venomous species, small mammals, birds, lizards, and frogs

(*Lampropeltis getula*)
Also called the "thunder snake," this shiny brown or black snake has smooth scales and a chainlike pattern of cream or white along its body. Eastern kingsnakes live in pine and hardwood forests in the mid-Atlantic and southeastern states. They often hide under logs and leaf litter. In the early morning and on warm evenings, they hunt for food and often swim in streams to catch water snakes. Kingsnakes mate sometime between March and June. Between May and August the females lay clutches of 3 to 24 creamy-white eggs.

Scarlet Kingsnake

Rough Green Snake
(Opheodrys aestivus)

This bright green snake lives in trees, bushes, and vines, and blends in with the background so well that you can hardly see it. Rough green snakes slither around by day in search of grasshoppers to eat. They are good swimmers and spend much time in and near the water. They mate and the female lays some 3 to 12 hard, smooth eggs sometime between June and August. The young hatch after 5 to 12 weeks and are at first greenish-gray.

(Lampropeltis triangulum elapsoides)
This colorful snake is not poisonous, but it looks very similar to the poisonous eastern coral snake on page 26. The kingsnake's yellow, red, and black rings are arranged in a different pattern than that of the coral snake. The scarlet kingsnake has yellow rings and red rings separated by black rings but, on the poisonous coral snake, the red and yellow bands touch. The scarlet kingsnake also has a red snout, not black. You will not often see one out in the open, except at night and after heavy rain. It prefers to hide under logs and tree bark, and is found in pine forests, tropical hardwood forests, and deciduous woodlands. Scarlet kingsnakes mate in spring. The female lays between 2 and 17 eggs in a rotting log in June or July; these eggs hatch around August or September.

Animal group: Reptile
Family: Colubrid snake
Size: 14–27 in (35–69 cm)
Eats small snakes, lizards,
small rodents, and small fish

Animal group: Reptile
Family: Colubrid snake
Size: 22–32 in (56–81 cm)
Eats grasshoppers,
crickets, caterpillars,
and spiders

Broadhead Skink
(Eumeces laticeps)

Like the five-lined skink, this skink also has five light stripes on its back, but its head is broader and its body is bigger. Broadhead skinks like moist woodlands with plenty of leaf litter. They often climb trees to hunt for insects to eat. They sometimes shake the nests of paper wasps, dislodge the wasp pupae, and eat them. The stings from the adult wasps as they try to protect their nest do not seem to hurt these skinks. They mate sometime around April or May. The female lays a clutch of 6 to 16 eggs sometime between May and July. The nest may be in a hole under a log or in leaf litter. She guards the eggs until they hatch sometime between June and August.
Animal group: Reptile
Family: Skink
Size: 6½–12¾ in (16.5–32 cm)
Eats insects and other
small invertebrates

Five-lined Skink
(Eumeces fasciatus)

This skink gets its name from the five wide, light-colored stripes on its body. As the skink grows older, these lines fade and may even disappear. In adults, the tail is usually blue to gray, and in the young it is bright blue. Breeding males have a bright orange head. Five-lined skinks prefer to live on the ground and climb trees only to bask in the sun. They like woodlands with logs, tree stumps, and plenty of leaf litter, but they also sometimes live in gardens and around buildings. Five-lined skinks mate in spring. The female lays between 4 and 15 eggs in a nest sometime around May or June. She tends the eggs until they hatch later in the summer.

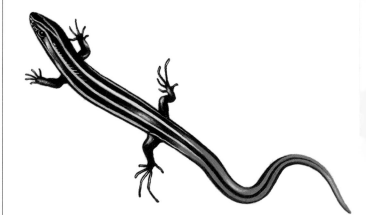

Animal group: Reptile
Family: Skink
Size: 5–8 in (12.5–20 cm)
Eats insects, spiders, earthworms,
lizards, crustaceans, and small mice

Western Fence Lizard

(Sceloporus occidentalis)
This spiny lizard has a dark-colored body with a pattern of matching patches or wavy bars along its back. Its scales are the same size all over. Its inside legs are yellowish-orange. Its belly is marked with blue, hence its nickname "blue belly." Adult males also have a blue patch on the throat. These lizards like mixed forests, as well as scrub and grassy areas, and you may spot them on fences and walls during the day. The western fence lizard mates in early spring. The female lays 3 to 14 eggs sometime between May and July.

Animal group: Reptile
Family: Iguanid
Size: 6–9 in (15–23 cm)
Eats insects and other small invertebrates

Wood Turtle

(Clemmys insculpta)
The upper shell of the wood turtle is very rough and looks as though it has been carved. The turtle's neck and front legs are often reddish-orange, which is why it is nicknamed "red leg." Wood turtles like cool streams in deciduous woodlands. They are excellent climbers and can even climb fences. Look for wood turtles after spring rains, as they search for worms to eat. The females lay one clutch of 6 to 8 eggs sometime between May and June; the eggs hatch around September or October.

Animal group: Reptile
Family: Pond and marsh turtles
Shell size: 5–9 in (12.5–23 cm)
Eats slugs, insects, tadpoles, worms, and wild berries
This is a protected species in some states.

Tadpole Fun

Tadpole, or polliwog, is the name given to an immature frog or toad. The adults often live far from water but return in spring to mate and to lay their eggs, usually in still water. The eggs, called spawn, are covered in a jellylike material.

Check with your teacher or an expert at a local nature center before doing these activities. The teacher or expert may recommend a different activity more appropriate for your locality. Nature activities can be harmful to animals or their environment, or to you, so always get expert advice and have an adult along on any expedition.

Collecting spawn and tadpoles

The best place to collect spawn is from a garden pond. Only collect from a "wild" pond if there is plenty there. Remember, it takes a great many tadpoles to produce just a few frogs because so many are eaten by fish, birds, and other predators.

1 **Collect about half a cup (120 milliliters) of spawn or a few dozen tadpoles** in a small net. Carry them home in a bucket. (Frog spawn is the easiest to find and keep.)
2 **Put the spawn into an aquarium** with tap water that has been allowed to stand for a day or two to get rid of the chlorine. Or, you can use pond water, if it is not too muddy.
3 **Add a few rocks and some water plants.** Cover the tank with netting or the birds will get a free meal.
4 **Place the aquarium in dappled shade.** Tadpoles like warm water, but they may die if left in sunshine.
5 **Your tadpoles will need feeding a few days after they hatch.** At this stage, they are plant-eaters. Add small pieces of boiled lettuce leaves and 4 or 5 pellets or rabbit food every 3 or 4 days. Not too much, or the uneaten food will foul the water.
6 **Change the water if it gets murky** and add more as it evaporates.

Metamorphosis

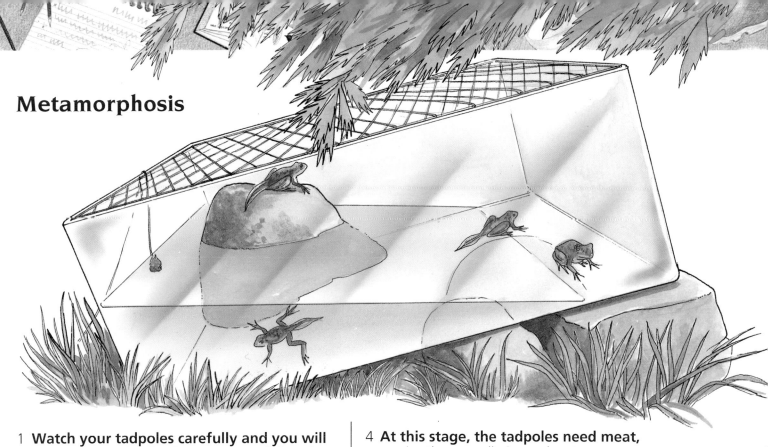

1 **Watch your tadpoles carefully and you will see them gradually change into adults.** This change is called metamorphosis (see page 4). Keep a diary of what happens. When do the hind and front legs first appear?

2 **If you can, record the temperature of the water in your tank on the same day once a week.** If you have two tanks, try keeping one in cool shade at about 60–65 °Fahrenheit (15–18 °Celsius). Keep the other tank in a warmer spot at about 70–75 °Fahrenheit (21–24 °Celsius). The tadpoles in the warmer water should grow more quickly.

3 **When the hind legs appear** (from about a week to several months after hatching), put some rocks in the tank so the tadpoles can climb out of the water. They will soon need to breathe air.

4 **At this stage, the tadpoles need meat,** so give them small pieces about once a week. Remove uneaten food after a couple of days or the water will get foul.

5 **When the tadpoles' front legs appear,** prop up the tank so that there is a shallow end, or build islands in the tank out of small stones.

6 **The small froglets or toadlets should be released in a damp corner of your yard** or around the edges of a pond. They are very difficult to feed at this stage and are better returned to nature. Carry them in a box lined with damp moss or grass. **They will drown if placed in a bucket of water.**

Streams & Rivers

Streams and rivers are perfect places to see amphibians and reptiles that like to live near moving water, because there are always plenty of insects for them to eat in these freshwater habitats. Some amphibians and reptiles prefer shallow, fast-moving streams, and others prefer slow, deep, mud-bottomed rivers. You are most likely to find the larger salamanders and reptiles—such as spiny softshells (turtles)—in large streams and rivers.

The smaller salamanders prefer springs and streams with fewer fish to prey on them or their young. These open stretches of fresh water are often shallow at the edges, and are full of rocks, pebbles, and plants that provide places to hide or to lay eggs. Some amphibians are able to attach their eggs to a rock in the water so that they are not washed away by the current. Salamanders like to live among rocks and leaf litter on a riverbank, and they lay their eggs under a rock, inside a rotting log, or in a hole in the soil.

This picture shows reptiles and amphibians from this section—how many do you recognize?

Clockwise from top left: spotted frog, foothill yellow-legged frog, Pacific giant salamander, western blackneck garter snake, and tailed frog.

Spotted Frog
(Rana pretiosa)

This big spotted frog has a reddish belly and a brown back with dark spots. Its face is darkly masked and there is a light stripe on its upper jaw. The male has extra large "thumbs" and is smaller than the female. These frogs live in mountainous areas, and they like cool streams and lakes without too much plant life in the water.

Animal group: Amphibian
Family: True frog
Size: 2–4 in (5–10 cm)
Feeds by day on small invertebrates

Canyon Tree Frog
(Hyla arenicolor)

With its plump body and rough, warty skin, this frog looks more like a toad. Canyon tree frogs are brown to olive with dark blotches. Look for them alongside rocky streams and rivers in the desert, especially in canyon bottoms. They spend most of their time on the ground and are well disguised. They are almost the same color and pattern as the rocks in their habitat.

Animal group: Amphibian
Family: Tree frog
Size: 1¼–2¼ in (3–5.75 cm)
Feeds at night on small invertebrates

Tailed Frog
(Ascaphus truei)

The tailed frog is usually olive or brown, with lots of dark spots and small warts. It lives in cool, clear, fast mountain streams. The female attaches her fertilized eggs to rocks in the water, and the tadpoles cling to these rocks using a sucker adapted for this purpose. The tadpoles take from six months to four years to turn into adult frogs. Tailed frogs do not have real tails; as is shown in the picture, however, the males have a taillike organ. In most species of frogs, the male fertilizes eggs after they are laid by the female. In the tailed frog, the male uses his taillike organ to fertilize the eggs while they are still inside the female.

Animal group: Amphibian
Family: Tailed frog
Size: 1–2 in (2.5–5 cm)
Tadpoles feed on algae and small invertebrates in the water, while adults feed on insects and other invertebrates

Foothill Yellow-legged Frog
(Rana boylii)

This frog is named for the yellow coloring on the underside of its legs. Yellow-legged frogs like gravelly or sandy streams with sunny banks and woodlands close by. If alarmed, they dive into the water and hide among the rocks at the bottom of the stream until the danger has passed. They mate in spring, and the females usually attach their eggs to rocks underwater.

Animal group: Amphibian
Family: True frog
Size: 1¾–3 in (4.5–7.5 cm)
Feeds on invertebrates

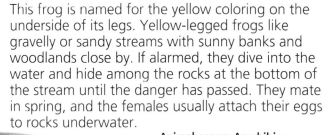

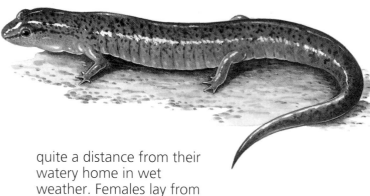

Northern Red Salamander
(Pseudotriton ruber ruber)

The plump northern red salamander is one of the easiest eastern salamanders to recognize, with its yellow eyes and bright reddish body covered with black spots. The young are usually coral-red or orange, and they become darker as they grow older. Adults can be orange-brown to purplish. These salamanders like cool, clear water, and you can find them in and around brooks, streams, and springs. See if you can spot a red salamander searching for food in leaf litter. They often wander quite a distance from their watery home in wet weather. Females lay from 50 to 100 eggs in nesting sites in early fall.

Animal group: Amphibian—Family: Lungless salamander
Size: 4–7 in (10–18 cm)—Feeds on earthworms

Pacific Giant Salamander

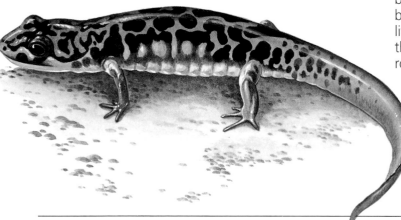

(Dicamptodon tenebrosus)
This big, smooth-skinned salamander is purplish or brown, mottled with black. Its belly is usually light brown to yellowish-white. Adult giant salamanders live in or around rivers and streams that flow through cool woodlands, where they hide under rocks, leaf litter, and logs. They breed in spring, and the females lay their eggs in water. The young live in water, where they eat insects and the tadpoles of tailed frogs.

Animal group: Amphibian
Family: Mole salamander—Size: 7–11¾ in (18–30 cm)
Adults feed on other salamanders,
garter snakes, large insects, and mice

Spring Salamander
(Gyrinophilus porphyriticus)

Animal group: Amphibian
Family: Lungless salamander—Size: 4¼–8¾ in (10.5–22 cm)
Sometimes hunts on land on wet nights for insects and smaller salamanders, but little is known of its habits

The spring salamander is named after the cool springs in the Appalachian Mountains where it lives, but you can also see it in mountain streams, hiding under rotting logs nearby, or in wet caves. It is one of the largest lungless salamanders and is pinkish-orange, patterned with darker markings. These salamanders breed during the warm summer months, and the female lays up to 100 eggs, one at a time, which she attaches to stones in the water.

Southern Two-lined Salamander

(Eurycea cirrigera)

Can you guess how this salamander got its name? A dark line runs from each eye to the tip of its tail. You may see one of these salamanders near a rocky brook or stream, but they will dash away to hide under leaf litter or a rock if alarmed. Female two-lined salamanders lay up to 100 eggs in the water under rocks, logs, or plants. Sometimes the female guards the eggs until they hatch.

Animal group: Amphibian
Family: Lungless salamander
Size: 2¼–4¾ in (5.75–12 cm)
Feeds on insects and other invertebrates

(Eurycea longicauda)

This pretty salamander is often yellow to orange-red with black spots on its body and V-shaped bars along its tail. The slim tail is very long, which makes it easy to tell this salamander apart from others. Long-tailed salamanders live in streams and springs in wooded areas. They breed sometime between the fall and spring, then the females lay their eggs in underground holes close to the stream where they live. They often come out on warm rainy nights to search for food on the forest floor.

Long-tailed Salamander

Animal group: Amphibian
Family: Lungless salamander—Size: 4–8 in (10–20 cm)
Feeds on tiny insects and other invertebrates

Dusky Salamander

(Desmognathus fuscus)

The dusky salamander lives in rocky woodland streams and creeks. The adults come in many colors and patterns, but they are usually tan or brown. The young have five to eight pairs of yellowish spots on their back. The tail is triangular in cross-section. Dusky salamanders breed in summer, and the female lays up to 36 eggs under rocks, in rotting logs, and in holes in stream banks.
Animal group: Amphibian
Family: Lungless salamander—Size: 2½–5½ in (6.5–14 cm)
Feeds on insect larvae, wood lice, and earthworms

Western Blackneck Garter Snake
(Thamnophis cyrtopsis cyrtopsis)

The blackneck garter snake is olive-gray or brown with a yellow stripe down the middle of its back and black patches behind its head. It lives in canyon and mountain streams and springs, and it swims along searching for prey. This snake is active during the day, and you may see one soaking up the sun on a rock. The females give birth to between 7 and 25 young in summer.

Animal group: Reptile—Family: Colubrid snake
Size: 16–43 in (40–110 cm)
Feeds on toads, frogs, and tadpoles

Greater Siren
(Siren lacertina)

With its long, thick, gray-green body and tiny legs, you could easily think this animal—one of the largest salamanders in North America—is an eel. The greater siren lives in shallow, muddy streams filled with weeds and, like the mudpuppy, keeps the gilled, larval form all its life. During the day, it lies buried in mud under rocks or water plants. If the stream where it lives dries up in summer, the siren keeps moist by producing extra slime from its skin glands, then coating its entire body with a thick layer of the slime, like a cocoon. Sirens can live for up to 25 years.

Animal group: Amphibian
Family: Siren
Size: 20–38 in (51–65 cm)
Feeds at night on snails, small fish, water plants, and insect larvae

Mudpuppy
(Necturus maculosus)

This large, water-dwelling salamander lives in rivers and streams, including muddy waters that are overgrown with weeds. It is gray to brown with dark blue spots, and its belly is gray with dark spots. A mudpuppy never turns into a land-dwelling, air-breathing adult, but it instead looks like a larva all its life, with feathery gills behind its head. Mudpuppies breed in spring. The female lays up to 190 eggs. She attaches them to a stone or log underwater, and she guards them until they hatch.

Animal group: Amphibian
Family: Mudpuppy and waterdog—Size: 8–17 in (20–43 cm)
Feeds at night on worms, crayfish, insects, and small fish

Spiny Softshell

(Apalone sinifera)

Instead of a hard, bonelike shell, this turtle has a soft shell made of thick, brown skin marked with round spots and a line around the edge. Apart from that, this turtle's long neck and tubelike snout can help you tell it apart from other turtles. Spiny softshells live in boggy ponds, rivers, and lakes. They like to sunbathe, but they can move quickly both on land and in water, so you will be lucky to see one up close in the wild.

Animal group: Reptile
Family: Softshell turtle
Shell size: Male is 5–9 in (12.5–23 cm)
Female is 6–18 in (15–45.5 cm)
Feeds on plants, small fish, and insects
WARNING: This turtle can give a painful bite!

Hellbender

(Cryptobranchus alleganiensis)

This huge, slimy salamander is brown or gray, looks flattened around the head and body, and has a flapping curtain of skin along both sides of its body. The hellbender spends its entire life in water, and it particularly likes rushing rivers with lots of flat stones on the riverbed under which it can hide. The male is smaller than the female, and in the breeding season he makes a nest under a flat rock or log. The female lays up to 500 eggs, and the male often guards them until the larvae hatch two or three months later. Hellbenders are also called "devil dogs" but, despite their fearsome names, they are completely harmless.

Animal group: Amphibian
Family: Giant salamander—Size: 12–29 in (30–73.5 cm)
Feeds on fish, snails, crayfish, and worms

Focus on snakes

People who have never handled a snake often think its skin will feel cold and slimy. In fact, snakes have dry, scaly, waterproof skins. Unlike you, snakes never stop growing and soon become too big for their skins. Young snakes shed their skins about every month or more in their first year, when they are growing fast. Adults change skins 2 to 3 times a year.

Snakebite prevention

Snakes bite to subdue or kill their prey so that they can eat it. Some will also bite in self-defense if frightened, stepped on, touched, or picked up. Given a chance, a snake will flee from you.

- **Never go alone to areas where there may be venomous snakes.**
- **Wear sturdy boots or shoes and thick trousers** in snake territory.
- **Be careful where you put your hands and feet.**
- **Carry a light when walking outside at night.**
- **Learn to recognize the poisonous species** and where they are found. Rattlesnakes, coral snakes, water moccasins, and copperheads are all poisonous.

First aid

- **If bitten, remain calm.** Snakebite, even from poisonous species, is rarely fatal. The snake may inject only a small amount of venom.
- **Lie down and send someone for help. Or walk slowly toward help.** Not moving or moving slowly will help to stop the spread of the venom in the blood. Keep as still as possible until you reach the doctor or hospital.
- **Try to remember what the snake looked like.** This will help the doctor to know which anti-venom to give you.
- **If you have learned first aid** and cannot get to a hospital within 30 minutes or so:
  1 Tie a band of cloth above the bite. The band must fit snugly but should be loose enough for someone to slip a finger beneath.
  2 Do not loosen the band until medical care is obtained.
  3 Do not take any aspirin or aspirin substitute containing acetaminophen or ibuprofen.

Snakeskin crafts

A shed snakeskin may look delicate, but it is actually quite tough. You can make interesting greeting cards, book marks, and pictures from it.

1 **Fold a piece of art paper to make a blank card.** Draw your favorite snake on it and color it in using bright colors.

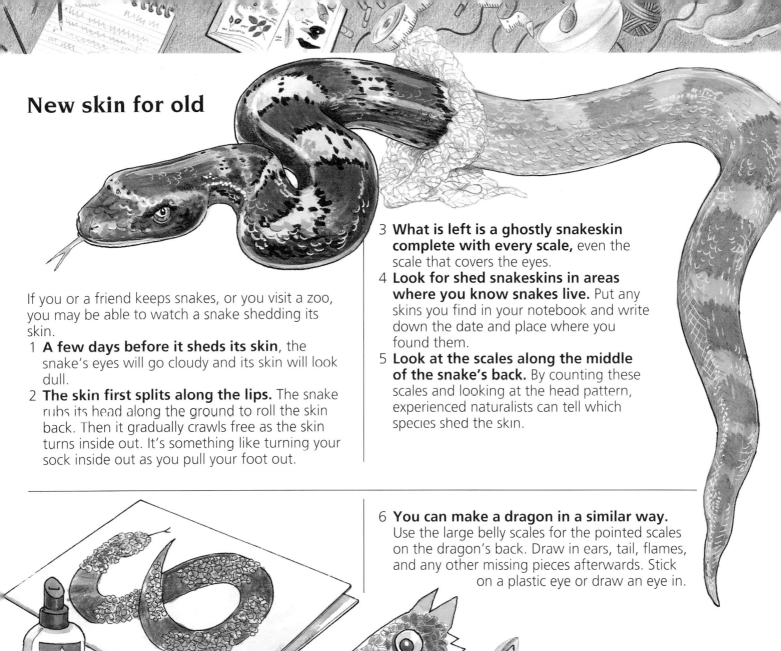

New skin for old

If you or a friend keeps snakes, or you visit a zoo, you may be able to watch a snake shedding its skin.

1 **A few days before it sheds its skin**, the snake's eyes will go cloudy and its skin will look dull.

2 **The skin first splits along the lips.** The snake rubs its head along the ground to roll the skin back. Then it gradually crawls free as the skin turns inside out. It's something like turning your sock inside out as you pull your foot out.

3 **What is left is a ghostly snakeskin complete with every scale,** even the scale that covers the eyes.

4 **Look for shed snakeskins in areas where you know snakes live.** Put any skins you find in your notebook and write down the date and place where you found them.

5 **Look at the scales along the middle of the snake's back.** By counting these scales and looking at the head pattern, experienced naturalists can tell which species shed the skin.

6 **You can make a dragon in a similar way.** Use the large belly scales for the pointed scales on the dragon's back. Draw in ears, tail, flames, and any other missing pieces afterwards. Stick on a plastic eye or draw an eye in.

2 **Lightly spread glue inside the snake's outline.** Be careful not to glue outside the lines.

3 **Stick pieces of snakeskin to the glue** and trim off the edges outside the snake's outline.

4 **Color in the background** if you want to.

5 **Cover the card with sticky plastic film** for protection.

Lakes, Ponds, & Marshes

A still, freshwater lake or pond is an ideal place to watch reptiles and amphibians that live in and around the water. The amphibian breeding season is usually from late winter to early spring in temperate areas or in the rainy season in subtropical regions, and at this time freshwater habitats ring with the mating calls of frogs. For many people, the first sign of spring is the shrill call of the peeper. Some reptiles and amphibians may live on the shore of a lake, while others live in the trees overhanging the water.

Ponds and lakes are also important to some reptiles and amphibians that spend the rest of the year in a different habitat, such as a nearby woodland. Spotted salamanders migrate each year to breeding pools to lay their eggs, then return at once to their other home in the woods.

Many amphibians breed in the temporary pools brought by spring rain or melted snow, even though these pools contain no fish or other food to eat. Other wetland habitats, such as marshes and the edges of ponds and lakes, are among the most threatened habitats in North America. Millions of acres of marsh, swamp, and bog have been drained, and many species of reptile and amphibian living there are now endangered.

This picture shows reptiles and amphibians from this section—how many do you recognize?

Clockwise from top left: green frog, mud turtle, spotted turtle, gray tree frog, and western ribbon snake.

Gray Tree Frog
(Hyla versicolor)

Gray tree frogs usually spend the day high in the branches of tall trees growing beside lakes, but they come down at night. Listen for their loud, trilling call during the breeding season in spring and early summer. These frogs have gray to greenish-gray coloring with large dark patches, which helps to disguise them against the bark of their treetop home. They have a pale spot rimmed with black below each eye, and their inner thighs are bright yellow or orange.
Animal group: Amphibian
Family: Tree frog
Size: 1¼–2½ in (3–6.5 cm)
Eats insects

Green Tree Frog
(Hyla cinerea)

This brilliant green frog has a pale stripe running from its upper jaw down the sides of its body. It is not always green; it may be yellow or greenish-gray. Occasionally, it has tiny gold dots on its back. These frogs often sleep under a large leaf or in other damp, shady places during the day. Green tree frogs gather together in huge groups to sing, and the males call while clinging to the stems of water plants. From a distance, their song sounds like a cow bell. These frogs like to walk rather than jump.

Animal group: Amphibian
Family: Tree frog
Size: 1¼–2½ in (3–6.5 cm)
Eats insects and other small invertebrates

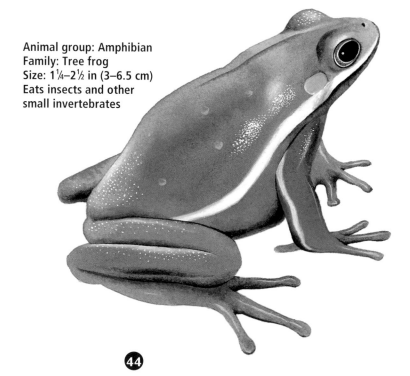

Northern Cricket Frog
(Acris crepitans)

This rough-skinned frog is active during the day. It has a black triangular mark on the forehead and is colored black, brown, green, yellow, or red. Cricket frogs can hop quite quickly even though their legs are short. They like shallow ponds with plenty of plant life and sunny, slow-moving streams, where they can sunbathe at the edge. Cricket frogs are so named because their song sounds like the call of a cricket.

Animal group: Amphibian
Family: Tree frog
Size: ½–1½ in (1–4 cm)
Eats insects and small invertebrates

Spring Peeper
(Pseudacris crucifer)

Although a chorus of these frogs is said to signal the beginning of spring, they sound more like sleigh bells jingling. Listen for them calling to each other from dead grass and the base of shrubs in woodland and meadow ponds. Spring peepers can be dark or light brown or gray and feature a big crosslike mark on the back. They live in wet woodlands and are out at night. In winter, they hibernate under logs and loose bark.

Animal group: Amphibian
Family: Tree frog
Size: ¾–1½ in (2–4 cm)
Eats insects and small invertebrates

Upland Chorus Frog
(Pseudacris triseriata feriarum)

These frogs love to sing; they make a scraping, grating sound. You may hear a chorus frog, but it would be unusual to see one in the wild, as they tend to hide and hop into the water at the slightest movement. Chorus frogs live in grassy areas near lakes, ponds, swamps, and rivers. They are brown, gray, or green, with smooth skin marked with lines. They also have a wide band running across each eye and down the side of the body, and a white line on their top jaw.

Animal group: Amphibian
Family: Tree frog—**Size:** ¾–1½ in (2–4 cm)
Eats insects and small invertebrates

Red-legged Frog
(Rana aurora)

During the day, you can see this big frog searching for food around ponds, lakes, and woodland areas. Its name stems from the red on the underside of its hind legs. Its back is reddish-brown to gray, with darker blotches and specks. Its belly is mainly yellow and darkens into red. There is usually a dark pattern like a mask on its face and a white line on its jaw. These frogs breed from January to March, and the females lay masses of eggs in the water.
Animal group: Amphibian
Family: True frog
Size: 2–5½ in (5–14 cm)
Eats insects and other small invertebrates

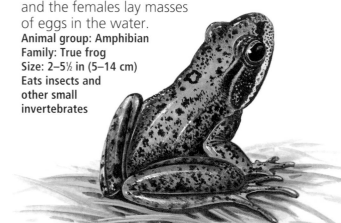

Pickerel Frog *(Rana palustris)*

This frog is smooth-skinned, with two rows of dark, square-shaped spots along its back. Its belly and the underside of its hind legs are a clear yellow-orange. It has a light stripe on its jaw. The pickerel frog likes to be near swamps and slow-moving streams. Its call is a low croak. Sometimes it croaks underwater and sounds as though it is snoring. It wards off enemies by releasing a stinging fluid from its skin.
Animal group: Amphibian
Family: True frog
Size: 1¾–3½ in (4.5–9 cm)
Eats insects and other small invertebrates
WARNING: Beware! Its stinging fluid can irritate your skin. Don't touch the pickerel frog.

(Rana clamitans)
This frog has two raised ridges on its back, one down each side. A green frog may be greenish-brown or bronze with brown blotches. Its belly is white with a pattern of lines or spots, and the males have a yellow throat. You can see green frogs in many parts of eastern North America. They like shallow ponds, lakesides, swamps, and marshes.
Animal group: Amphibian
Family: True frog
Size: 2¼–4 in (5.75–10 cm)
Hunts at night for insects and other small invertebrates

Green Frog

Western Toad
(Bufo boreas)

This big, warty toad is grayish-green, with a cream stripe down the center of its back. Its reddish warts are surrounded by black blotches. Western toads like damp areas in woodlands, alpine meadows, arid scrub, and low grasslands. They live in a burrow that they make themselves, or in the abandoned burrow of another animal, such as a mouse. Listen for their call, a sound like the "peep-peep" of baby chicks.

Animal group: Amphibian
Family: True toad
Size: 2½–5 in (6.5–12.5 cm)
Eats insects and other small invertebrates

Bullfrog
(Rana catesbeiana)

Listen for the bullfrog's call. It sounds like "jug o'rum" and will carry for a long way on a still day. The bullfrog's length of 8 inches (20 centimeters) makes it one of the largest frogs in North America. Its body varies in color from yellow to green and is sometimes marked with yellow or gray. Its belly is white and might have brown patches, as well. It has large, visible eardrums behind each eye, which are often larger than the eye itself. Bullfrogs like spacious stretches of water to move around in, with enough foliage to give good cover. They are active at night—then you might see them on the banks of lakes and ponds. If they are alarmed, they hop into the undergrowth or into the water. Bullfrog tadpoles may take up to two years to turn into adults.

Animal group: Amphibian
Family: True frog
Size: Up to 8 in (20 cm)
Eats other frogs, insects, crayfish, and sometimes small birds and snakes

Lakes, Ponds, & Marshes

Northern Water Snake

(Nerodia sipedon)

You can see this snake around lakes, ponds, rivers, ditches, and bogs. It may be out during the day or at night searching for food. It also likes to bask in the sun. The northern water snake is brownish or gray with darker patches on its back and sides, and dark bands in the neck area. Its belly is light and often marked with a jumble of reddish half-moon shapes. These snakes mate in late spring, and the females give birth to up to 30 young in late summer to early fall. This snake is not venomous, but it is easily confused with the water moccasin (see page 52), which has a deadly bite.

Animal group: Reptile
Family: Colubrid snake
Size: 24–42 in (60–107 cm)
Eats salamanders, turtles, frogs, and small fish

Red-spotted Newt

(Notophthalmus viridescens viridescens)
This is the adult of the colorful red eft on page 19. The adults live in water, whereas the efts live on land. Red-spotted newts are yellowish-brown or olive-green, with red spots edged with black on their back. They live in and around ponds, small lakes, marshes, and streams. These newts breed from late winter to early spring. The females lay between 200 and 400 eggs, one at a time, on water plants.

Animal group: Amphibian
Family: Newt—Size: Up to 4 in (10 cm)
Eats worms, crustaceans, insects, and mollusks

Diamondback Water Snake

(Nerodia rhombifer)

This snake is named after the dark brown, chainlike pattern on its lighter brown back. It is active by day, and you may spot one basking on a log on the edge of a lake, pond, river, stream, swamp, or ditch. Diamondback water snakes mate in spring, and the females give birth to up to some 60 young between August and October. These snakes are not venomous, but they are aggressive and quick to bite. They can be confused with the water moccasin (see page 52).

Animal group: Reptile
Family: Colubrid snake
Size: 30–63 in (76–160 cm)
Eats fish and frogs

American Alligator

(Alligator mississippiensis)

The alligator's tough, knobbly skin is mostly dark olive or gray. A young animal will have lighter bands across its body. Commonly reaching 9 to 12 feet, it is North America's biggest reptile. It has a wide snout. Alligators live in the lakes, swamps, bayous, ponds, and marshes of the southeast coast from North Carolina to Texas, and several hundred miles inland. They hibernate in winter, then come out of their den in spring to breed. You can hear males bellowing to each other from a long way off. The female lays her eggs in a nest of mud and leaves and stays close until the young hatch about nine weeks later. American alligators look after their young for one to three years. Once an endangered species, the alligator is now common in many areas.

Animal group: Reptile—Family: Crocodile
Size: 9–12 ft (2.7–3.7 m)
Eats fish, crustaceans, and insects (when young), as well as birds, snakes, frogs, and small mammals

Red-eared Slider

(Trachemys scripta elegans)

This pretty turtle is easy to recognize because, as its name suggests, it has red marks behind each eye that look like little red ears. Red-eared sliders enjoy basking in the sun, and you can often see a crowd of them piled on top of each other on a favorite log. They live in ponds, lakes, swamps, slow rivers, and shallow streams. They mate sometime from March to June and lay one to three clutches of up to 23 eggs each in a hole in the ground. These turtles are also called "pond sliders."

Animal group: Reptile
Family: Pond and marsh turtles
Shell size: 5–11½ in (12.5–29.5 cm)
The young eat tadpoles, water insects, crustaceans, and mollusks; they start eating plants as they grow older

Spotted Turtle
(Clemmys guttata)

The spotted turtle is one of the prettiest turtles and one of the easiest to recognize. Its shell is black with a pattern of yellow dots. Females have orange eyes and a yellow chin, and males have brown eyes, a tan chin, and a long, thick tail. Spotted turtles mate in early spring; in early summer the female lays up to eight eggs in a shallow nest that she digs in a sunny place. Look for these turtles in early spring sitting on logs at the edge of ponds and shallow-bottomed streams.
Animal group: Reptile—Family: Pond and marsh turtles
Shell size: 3½–5 in (9–12.5 cm)—Eats insects and water plants

Common Musk Turtle
(Sterotherus odoratus)

This turtle is also known as "stinkpot" and "stinking Jim" because, when it is disturbed, it produces a nasty-smelling fluid from glands near its hind legs. The turtle has two pale lines on its head and a green, brown, or dark gray shell; the shell is sometimes green with algae. It lives in shallow waters. You may spot one in spring, sunbathing in the water with the top of its shell in the sun. They also climb trees to reach the sun. Musk turtles mate underwater. The females lay three to nine eggs in a shallow nest on the pond bank or beneath rotting logs.
Animal group: Reptile—Family: Musk and mud turtles
Shell size: 3–5½ in (7.5–14 cm)—Eats snails, clams, and other invertebrates, as well as aquatic plants
WARNING: The males are quick to bite.

(Kinosternon subrubrum hippocrepis)
This turtle lives in overgrown swamps and ponds. As its name would suggest, the mud turtle spends most of its time on the muddy bottom of its watery home. If the water in the pond or swamp dries up, the turtle can burrow into the mud and survive there until it rains and the water returns. A mud turtle's shell is olive to dark brown and smooth on top, and it is yellow to brown below. Males have a blunt spine at the end of the tail. During the summer, these turtles spend more time on land. They breed in spring, and the female lays one to six eggs in a hole that she digs in the soil. These turtles sometimes lay their eggs in abandoned muskrat or beaver lodges.

Mississippi Mud Turtle

Animal group: Reptile
Family: Musk and mud turtles
Shell size: 3–5 in (7.5–12.5 cm)
Eats a variety of invertebrates and aquatic plants

Western Painted Turtle

(Chrysemys picta bellii)

Painted turtles are the most widespread turtles in North America, and the western painted turtle is the biggest subspecies. The top of its smooth, slightly flattened, oval shell is olive or black with red bars. The underside is yellow, and there are yellow stripes on its neck, legs, and tail. These turtles live in sluggish water in shallow streams, lakes, and rivers, and they like to sunbathe on logs in large groups. They nest in early summer and the females lay one or two clutches of eggs in northern areas, and two to four in southern regions.

Animal group: Reptile
Family: Pond and marsh turtles
Shell size: 4–10 in (10–25.5 cm)
Eats small fish, tadpoles, frogs, and water plants

Snapping Turtle

(Chelydra serpentina)

The huge head and long, tooth-edged tail will help you to spot this turtle. Snapping turtles like to be in warm, shallow, muddy water with lots of plant life, and they often bury themselves up to their eyes in mud. They mate from April to November, and the females lay up to 80 eggs in a hole in the ground a few weeks later. Snapping turtles are very good swimmers.

Animal group: Reptile
Family: Snapping turtle
Shell size: Up to 19 in (47 cm)
Eats fish, birds, small mammals, water plants, invertebrates, and carrion (previously killed animals)
WARNING: This turtle has strong jaws and a vicious bite, so keep well clear.

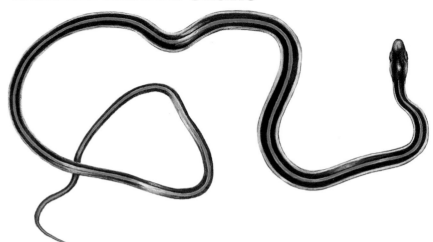

Western Ribbon Snake

(Thamnophis proximus)
Slim and ribbonlike, this garter snake slithers among the weeds at the water's edge, searching for food. It is dark in color with three light stripes running along its body. After mating in the spring, as many as 25 young may be born in mid- to late summer. Many of the young are eaten by predators.
Animal group: Reptile
Family: Colubrid snake
Size: 19–48½ in (48–123 cm)
Eats small fish, frogs, and tadpoles

Water Moccasin
(Agkistrodon piscivorus)

The **dangerous** water moccasin is also called the cottonmouth, because it throws back its head and displays its white-lined mouth as a warning signal. The water moccasin is the only water snake to swim with its head above the water. A heavy-looking, dark colored snake, it has a wide, flat top to its head and may have a brown stripe on each side of its face. Female water moccasins give birth to up to 15 young in late summer, after mating in the spring. You can spot the young water moccasins easily because of their yellow tails. They live in many different water habitats, from ditches to mountain streams.
Animal group: Reptile
Family: Pit viper—Size: 42–60 in (108–150 cm)
Hunts at night for frogs, fish, snakes, and birds
WARNING: Avoid this aggressive snake; its bite is very poisonous and can kill you!

Wandering Garter Snake
(Thamnophis elegans vagrans)

You may see this snake sunbathing in the morning at the edge of ponds, lakes, and streams. It also lives in damp meadows, open grassland, and forests near water. It has an indistinct yellowish-brown stripe and dark spots along its back. Wandering garter snakes hunt during the day. They mate in spring, and the females give birth to between 4 and 19 young sometime from July to September.
Animal group: Reptile
Family: Colubrid snake
Size: 18–42 in (45.5–108 cm)
Eats frogs, slugs, tadpoles, fish, worms, and small birds

Queen Snake
(Regina septemvittata)

A strong swimmer, the queen snake can be active by day or night. It is olive-brown to dark brown, with a yellowish stripe along the sides of its body and four brown stripes on its yellow belly. Queen snakes are found in many water habitats, including the edges of cool lakes; fast-flowing streams; small, rocky rivers; and sandy-bottomed creeks. They mate sometime between April and May, and females give birth to up to 23 young in late summer. You may spot a queen snake sunbathing on a tree branch overhanging the water. But if it notices you, it will drop into the water below and disappear in a flash.

Animal group: Reptile
Family: Colubrid snake
Size: 16–36¾ in (40–92 cm)
Eats mainly crayfish

Massasauga
(Sistrurus catenatus)

This **dangerous** snake lives in swamps around estuaries—the mouths of rivers—and that's where it got its name: "massasauga" means "river mouth" in the Chippewa language. They are also found in bogs, marshlands, flood plains, and grassy wetlands. The massasauga is a type of rattlesnake. It differs from other rattlesnakes by having nine large scales on the top of its head. Its body has dark blotches in a regular pattern, and it has a dark stripe going from its eye to the back of its neck. Mating season for this snake is from April to May, and females give birth to up to 19 young sometime between July and September. You may see one of these snakes basking in the sun on mild days.

Animal group: Reptile—Family: Pit viper
Size: 18–39½ in (45.5–99 cm)
Eats frogs, lizards, and small rodents
WARNING: While not as venomous as some rattlesnakes, the massasauga can deliver a dangerous bite if provoked. Do not approach this snake!

Keeping Lizards

Lizards can make fascinating pets. You will learn a lot and have fun caring for them. Given the right living conditions, they will live happily for many years.

Before you get any pet, learn as much as you can about the animal that interests you. Find out how much care it will need and how much its care will cost. You will be taking responsibility for a living thing that will rely entirely on you for its proper care throughout its life.

Equipment

Here is a list of some of the things you will need to keep a lizard. Check at your library or on reliable Internet sites for more information.

Try to make your lizard's home as similar to its natural habitat as possible, but also make sure you can observe your pet easily. You will need:

1 **A glass or plastic aquarium at least 30 inches (76 centimeters) long and 12 inches (30 centimeters) wide.** Buy a bigger one if you can. Secondhand will do, because it doesn't have to be leakproof. Later, if your pet succeeds in charming your family, you may want to build a larger terrarium!

2 **A sturdy lid to prevent escapes and to support lights (see below).** Strong wire mesh may do, but it must be firmly held down. It should be hinged or otherwise easy to remove.

3 **Your lizard will need two kinds of light.** An ultraviolet (UV) light for health (buy one made especially for reptiles) and a basking light for warmth.

4 **A thermometer and possibly a heater.**

5 **Places to hide and climb.** Ask your local pet store about options that are safe for your pet.

6 **Cover the floor of the tank with 1–2 inches (2.5–5 centimeters) of fine sand or smooth gravel.** Or, you can use pine bark mulch or shredded bark and soil (called orchid bark mix).

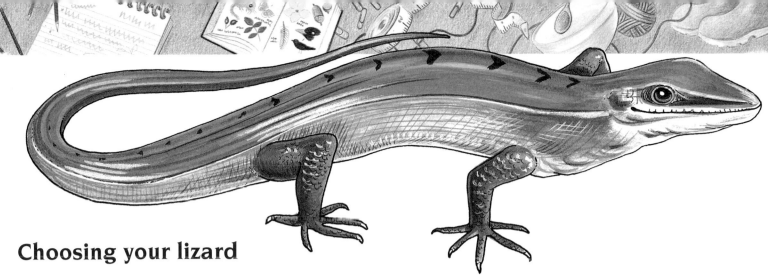

Choosing your lizard

Wild lizards should be left free. They have families and homes. You will have more fun watching them than catching them. They may also have parasites and be difficult to tame.

1 **Go to a reputable dealer and ask for captive-bred lizards.** These have not been taken from the wild and are used to living in captivity. Find out as much as possible about your chosen species before buying it.
2 **For your first lizard, choose a relatively cheap, hardy lizard.** Find out which species are easiest to keep. A healthy, lively, small brown lizard is a better choice than a brightly colored, exotic species that dies after a few weeks.

3 **There are many North American species that make good pets.** If you choose a "foreigner," make sure you can provide it with the right living conditions.
4 **You only need one.** Most lizards are territorial and will fight each other in a confined space.
5 **Make sure that the animal you buy has been well looked after** in the store. Otherwise it may soon die from shock and stress. You might check with a local veterinarian for a recommendation of a dealer.
6 **Check whether you need a permit to keep your lizard pet.**

Gecko guests

Some people who have pet geckos do not cage these animals. Instead, they allow the geckos to run freely throughout their houses! The geckos do no harm and are expert bug catchers! Mosquitoes, flies, and moths will disappear while the families sleep! You can watch geckos:

• **Run up walls and along ceilings.** They do this using special pads on their toes. The pads are made up of overlapping flaps covered in microscopic (tiny) hairlike bristles. These are so small they can grip on to the tiniest irregularity. If you can find a gecko climbing up glass, you will be able to look at the underside of its feet.

• **Shed their skin:** Lizard skin flakes off in large pieces.
• **Catch a fly:** They have huge eyes to help them see prey such as flies in the dark.

Grasslands

Grasslands stretch across the middle of the United States, from the Midwest, south to Texas and west to the Rockies. These grasslands then extend north into Canada. Grasslands feature large areas of long or short grass where crops can grow and animals can graze. Habitats like these are found in the Great Plains, the prairies, and some meadow areas in the East and West.

Ground-dwelling reptiles and amphibians that can survive hot, dry summers live in this habitat. Many of them find protection from predators and the sun by living underground. There are hardly any trees in these grasslands, but the grass provides shelter. Some animals, such as the smooth green snake (page 63), are so well camouflaged that they are almost invisible.

This picture shows reptiles and amphibians from this section—how many do you recognize?

Clockwise from top right: western skink, long-toed salamander, prairie rattlesnake, smooth green snake, and six-lined racerunner.

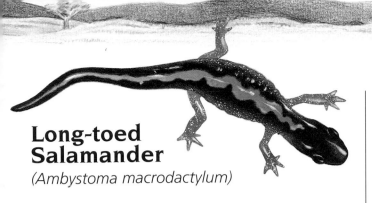

Long-toed Salamander
(Ambystoma macrodactylum)

This slender salamander lives in grassland areas under logs, tree bark, or rocks, close to lakes and streams. It may also be found in evergreen forests and mountain meadows. It is dark brown to black on top, with a light, blotchy stripe along its back. It breeds in ponds and rain pools from as early as January in warm regions to June in cooler regions. The female lays eggs, often one at a time, near the water's surface. The young are only about ½ inch (1 centimeter) long when they hatch; they turn into adults when they are 2–4 inches (5–10 centimeters) long.
Animal group: Amphibian
Family: Mole salamander—Size: 2½–4½ in (6.5–11.5 cm)
Feeds on insects and small invertebrates

Plains Spadefoot
(Spea bombifrons)

This chubby, gray-brown frog has a bump between its eyes and a black, horny projection called a *spade* on the inner surface of each hind foot. You can find these frogs in fields and shortgrass prairies. They like sandy soil. Listen for their call, which sounds like a quacking duck. They breed in summer when it rains. The female lays a mass of eggs and attaches it to a plant stem in a shallow pool or puddle. The eggs hatch into tadpoles within 48 hours. The tadpoles usually eat algae but may become carnivorous and eat each other. Those that survive grow into adults within two months.
Animal group: Amphibian
Family: Spadefoot
Size: 1½–2½ in (4–6.5 cm)
Hunts at night for insects and other invertebrates

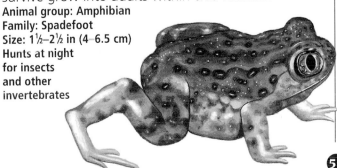

Western Chorus Frog
(Pseudacris triseriata)

You can hear this frog croaking on warm spring evenings. It can be found in prairies, woodlands, swamps, and farms. The males sit on floating plant leaves and call to the females, making a noise that sounds like a finger run across a pocket comb. In warm areas, these frogs breed in very early spring, but in cooler regions they wait until midsummer. Chorus frogs are smooth-skinned and are usually greenish-gray or brown, with three dark stripes down the back.
Animal group: Amphibian—Family: Tree frog
Size: ¾–1½ in (2–4 cm)
Hunts at night for small invertebrates

Great Plains Toad
(Bufo cognatus)

This large toad is gray to olive-brown and covered in dark blotches with light edges. It is active mainly at night, but you may see it searching for food by day in rainy weather. They are popular with farmers because this animal's favorite food is cutworms, which eat farm crops. If threatened, this toad puffs out its body, closes its eyes, and puts its head close to the ground; it then looks more like a stone than a toad. Great Plains toads breed from April to September, during or after heavy rain. The female lays a string of eggs at the bottom of a puddle.
Animal group: Amphibian
Family: True toad
Size: 2–4½ in (5–11.5 cm)
Eats insects and other small invertebrates
WARNING: This toad produces a poisonous substance from its skin. If you touch it, wash your hands thoroughly.

Grasslands

Collared Lizard
(Crotaphytus collaris)

One of the most striking of all lizards is this collared lizard, with its black-and-white collar and colorful yellow, brown, or green-blue body. The mature male has a yellow or orange throat (sometimes blue in subspecies that live in the West). When escaping from a predator, the collared lizard lifts up its tail and rushes along on its hind legs. Look for one jumping from rock to rock on rocky and sandy plains, as it chases after prey. These lizards also like to bask in the sun on boulders. Some live in forested areas. They breed from April to June and the females lay 1 to 12 eggs in midsummer.

Animal group: Reptile
Family: Iguanid
Size: 8–14 in (20–35 cm)
Feeds on insects and other lizards
WARNING: This lizard has strong jaws and will bite if provoked.

Lesser Earless Lizard
(Holbrookia maculata)

This small lizard usually has rows of dark blotches separated by a lighter stripe along the center of its back. The male has two black bars behind its front legs, and the female has an orange throat in the breeding season. The lesser earless lizard has long legs and toes, and no external ear openings, which is why it can so speedily burrow headfirst into the sand to hide. These lizards live on sandy prairies and are active during the day. When the sun is at its hottest, however, they stay in the shade or in the burrow of another animal. They breed in spring and summer and lay five to seven eggs.

Animal group: Reptile—Family: Iguanid
Size: 4–5¼ in (10–13 cm)—Feeds on small spiders and insects

(Cnemidophorus sexlineatus)
The only whiptail lizard in the eastern United States, this racerunner is brown and has six or seven light stripes. It looks like a skink, but its skin is not as shiny. Males have a green or blue throat, and females have a white throat. Racerunners are well named because they can usually outrun a predator; they are nicknamed "field streaks" because of their speed. These lizards are most active on warm mornings, when you can see them hunting or basking in the sun. At night and in cool weather, they burrow in the sand. They live in dry, sunny grasslands and open woodlands. They mate in spring and early summer; the female lays two clutches of eggs.

Six-lined Racerunner

Animal group: Reptile
Family: Whiptail lizard
Size: 6–10½ in (15–26.5 cm)
Feeds on insects and other small invertebrates

Short-horned Lizard
(Phrynosoma douglassii)

The short-horned lizard is quite easy to recognize by the crown of short spines on its head. You can tell this lizard apart from the Texas horned lizard (see page 72), because it has one row of spines along each side of its body instead of two. It lives on rocky and sandy plains, and you are most likely to see it during the warmest part of the day. After dark it burrows underground to sleep. The female gives birth to between 6 and 31 young in summer. These lizards are quite hardy and can survive cooler temperatures than can other species of horned lizards.

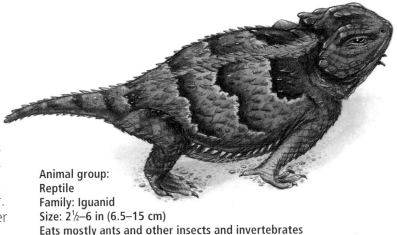

Animal group:
Reptile
Family: Iguanid
Size: 2½–6 in (6.5–15 cm)
Eats mostly ants and other insects and invertebrates

Western Skink
(Eumeces skiltonianus)

This skink has a brown stripe bordered by light stripes down its back from head to tail. During the mating season, the male has orange patches on the sides of his head and the tip of his tail. The western skink lives in rocky grassland areas and is active by day but tends to hide under stones, dead leaves, and logs. The female lays a clutch of two to six eggs in summer, which she cares for until they hatch. The young have bright blue tails.

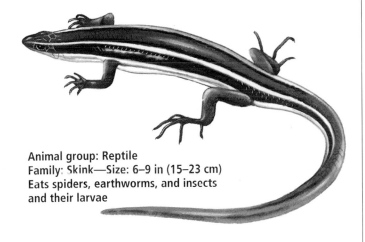

Animal group: Reptile
Family: Skink—Size: 6–9 in (15–23 cm)
Eats spiders, earthworms, and insects
and their larvae

Great Plains Skink
(Eumeces obsoletus)

This is the largest skink in the United States, and it lives on rocky grasslands. It has smooth scales and is sometimes patterned with indistinct stripes. The young are jet black with orange and white spots on the head and a bright blue tail. You will be lucky to see one because they often hide under rocks. They mate in spring, and the females lay some 7 to 21 eggs in a nest under a rock. The females watch over the eggs until they hatch in summer.

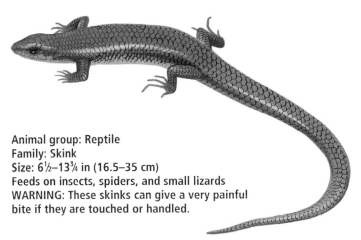

Animal group: Reptile
Family: Skink
Size: 6½–13¾ in (16.5–35 cm)
Feeds on insects, spiders, and small lizards
WARNING: These skinks can give a very painful bite if they are touched or handled.

Grasslands

Western Coachwhip
(Masticophis flagellum testaceus)

This large, long-tailed snake is possibly the fastest snake in the United States. It is usually pink, olive, yellow, or light brown above, with very little patterning. It slithers around during the day searching for food. If this snake is threatened, it may climb a tree or dart into a mammal's burrow. If cornered, it coils itself up, vibrates its tail, and strikes at the attacker. Western coachwhips like dry, open grasslands. They mate in spring, and the females lay clutches of some 4 to 16 eggs in summer.

Animal group: Reptile
Family: Colubrid snake—Size: 36–102 in (91.5–259 cm)
Eats other snakes, lizards, grasshoppers, birds, and small rodents
WARNING: Never corner this snake; it may strike and bite.

Striped Whipsnake
(Masticophis taeniatus)

Animal group: Reptile
Family: Colubrid snake
Size: 30–74 in (76.5–188 cm)
Eats lizards, birds, small mammals, and snakes

This long, slim snake is alert and fast-moving and, if surprised, it will speed into a mammal burrow or hide under rocks. It usually has two or more white or cream stripes along each side of its body, which make it easier to spot. The striped whipsnake hunts by day. It climbs trees in search of young birds to eat or to find a place to sunbathe. This snake lives in open pine and oak woodlands and rugged, mountainous areas. Striped whipsnakes mate in spring and may make a nest in an old mammal burrow. The female lays some 3 to 12 eggs in summer.

Checkered Garter Snake

(Thamnophis marcianus)

Patterned like a checkerboard, this snake likes dry grassland areas close to flowing water. It is active by day, when it hunts for food. The females give birth to some 6 to 18 young in summer. You are still likely to see this snake in the Southwest of the United States, but it is disappearing from other areas.

Animal group: Reptile
Family: Colubrid snake—Size: 18–42½ in (45–107 cm)
Eats frogs, fish, and crayfish

Plains Blackhead Snake

Animal group: Reptile
Family: Colubrid snake—Size: 7–14½ in (18–36 cm)
Feeds at night on centipedes, millipedes, spiders, and insects

(Tantilla nigriceps)
You can identify this snake by its black head, white belly, and unpatterned body. This is a shy snake that lives in prairies, desert grasslands, and woods. It sometimes shelters in burrows or under flat rocks in hilly areas. The female lays clutches of one to three eggs in spring or summer.

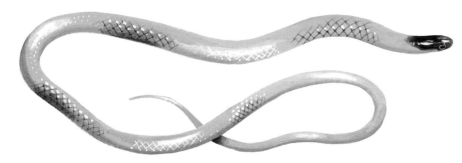

Bullsnake

(Pituophis catenifer sayi)

This powerfully built snake is usually yellow with about 40 brown blotches along its body. It is active during the day, and it often shelters in the burrow of a mammal or tortoise at night. If confronted, a bullsnake hisses loudly, then lunges at its intruder. Bullsnakes mate in spring, and the females lay up to 24 eggs in a burrow in sandy soil, or under a big rock or log. The young are about 12 to 18 inches (30–45 centimeters) long when they hatch.

Animal group: Reptile
Family: Colubrid snake
Size: 50–72 in (127–183 cm)
Feeds mainly on rodents, such as rats and mice
WARNING: Do not corner this snake or it may strike at you.

Grasslands

Great Plains Rat Snake

(Elaphe gutatta emoryi)
This snake is related to the colorful corn snake (see page 25), but it is gray with brown blotches. It has a mark shaped like a spearhead between its eyes and stripes under the tail. The Great Plains rat snake hides during the day under stones and in rock crevices—it then comes out at night to hunt. These snakes are found in rocky outcroppings and in grassland areas. They also live near rivers, streams, meadows, and in abandoned buildings.
Animal group: Reptile—Family: Colubrid snake
Size: 24–72 in (60–183 cm)
Eats rats, mice, birds, and bats

Eastern Yellow-bellied Racer
(Coluber constrictor flaviventris)

With its green coloring, this snake is easily mistaken for a smooth green snake (see next page), especially when young. It is a fast, agile snake that can climb well. It hunts for food during the day—speeding along with its head held high off the ground. Like other racers, these snakes mate in spring and the females lay their eggs in summer under a rock or in a mammal's abandoned burrow. Sometimes several females lay their eggs in the same nest. If annoyed, a racer may mimic the sound of a rattlesnake by rustling its tail in dead leaves. These snakes often hibernate in large groups.

Animal group: Reptile
Family: Colubrid snake
Size: 30–50 in (76–127 cm)
Eats large insects, frogs, lizards, other snakes, rodents, and birds

Prairie Rattlesnake
(Crotalus viridis viridis)

This **fierce and dangerous** snake has two light lines on its head and blotches along the back of its body. It lives in the grasslands of the Great Plains, and during the winter it shelters deep underground. It mates in spring and fall, and the female gives birth to between 4 and 21 young in late summer to fall.

Animal group: Reptile
Family: Pit viper
Size: 35–45 in (88–115 cm)
Adults feed mostly on small mammals, including rodents and prairie dogs, and the young eat lizards and mice
WARNING: Avoid this venomous snake! It is extremely dangerous.

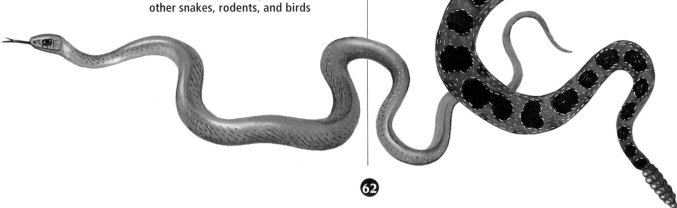

Ornate Box Turtle

(Terrapene ornata)

Animal group: Reptile
Family: Pond and marsh turtles
Shell size: 4–5 in (10–12.5 cm)
Eats earthworms, caterpillars, grasshoppers, beetles, berries, leaves, and carrion

This turtle has a hinged lower shell, so it can shut itself inside completely if danger threatens. These turtles are found in gently rolling prairies with sandy soil, especially on a sunny morning after rain. By midday, these turtles find a shady place to rest out of the sun. Look for disturbed piles of cow dung, as this could be where a box turtle has been digging for beetles and other insects. The female lays two to eight eggs in summer in a hole that she digs in the soil. The young hatch about 10 weeks later. Male box turtles have red eyes and females have yellow-brown eyes.

Smooth Green Snake

Animal group: Reptile
Family: Colubrid snake
Size: 14–26 in (35–66 cm)
Eats spiders and insects

(Opheodrys vernalis)
You will need sharp eyesight to spy this beautiful, bright green snake as it slithers through the grass. It is small and streamlined, with a long tail, and it is perfectly disguised in its grassland home. The females lay 3 to 11 eggs in late summer. Sometimes several females lay their eggs in the same hole in the ground.

Tracks, Trails, & Calls

Dusk chorus

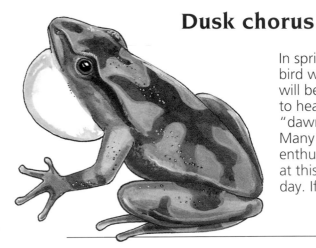

In spring, keen bird watchers will be up early to hear the "dawn chorus." Many birds sing enthusiastically at this time of day. If you go out in the early evening, just as the sun is setting, you may hear another chorus, this time made by frogs and toads. For instance, the chorus of the little spring peeper tree frog is familiar to many as a sign of spring. In spring, the males call loudly to impress and attract females to mate with them. They also try to frighten smaller males with the loudness of their croak. The croak is made by pumping air in and out of a large balloonlike structure under the chin, called a "vocal sac."

Making recordings

Frogs and toads have distinctive calls. With practice, you can learn to identify the species just from its call. Try taking a small tape recorder out with you.
1 **Record the date, time, and place** of your search on the tape.
2 **Locate the animals by following their croaks.** Move slowly and quietly, stopping to listen now and then.
3 **When you are quite near, record the sounds.**
4 **Now try to find the animals**. If you are lucky, you may catch a toad in the beam of your flashlight. Make a record on the tape of which species you think it is, or describe what you see.
You can also buy tapes of animal calls and learn from them. Newts and salamanders do not call, but many lizards do. Listen for the calls of geckos, which range from cricketlike chirps to loud barks.

Making an impression

A good way to study animal tracks is to make a plaster-cast impression of them. Try making casts from a pet's footprints and compare them with those you find in the wild.

1 **Buy a bag of plaster of Paris** from a drugstore or craft shop.
2 **Cut out some strips of thin cardboard** about 12 inches (30 centimeters) long and 2 inches (5 centimeters) wide.

3 **Look for a clear track,** preferably away from grass and other plants.
4 **Bend the cardboard into a circle that will fit around the footprint.** Secure with a paper clip. For a long track, try making an oblong shape.
5 **Push the cardboard circle a little way down into the mud or sand.**
6 **Pour about 2 fl. oz (50 milliliters) of water into a small container.** Add some plaster of Paris and stir with a stick or old teaspoon. The mixture needs to be like thick cream. With practice, you will soon find out how much you need for a cast.

7 **Pour the mixture into your cardboard circle** until it fills the footprint plus about ½ inch (1 centimeter) on top.
8 **Leave it alone until it sets.** This will take 15 to 20 minutes depending on the weather.
9 **Carefully pick up the cast** and peel off the cardboard surround.
10 **When the cast has dried completely, brush off dirt with an old toothbrush.** You can paint the footprint and the surrounding cast in different colors.

Remember, your cast will have lumps where the track had dents and vice versa!

Tracks and trails

The footprints of amphibians and reptiles are not as familiar as those of mammals and birds. But you can often tell what sort of animal has walked over an area, even if you can't tell the exact species. Learning to identify tracks and trails takes a lot of practice. Look in the mud around ponds for frog and toad tracks and turtle trails. In sandy areas and desert country, look for lizard prints and trails made by sidewinder snakes. Large tortoises leave clear footprints if they tread in mud or damp sand.

Sea turtles leave wide, tanklike tracks on sandy beaches (look for them on the Florida and Gulf coasts and beside tropical waters).

Deserts & Arid Scrub

The hot, dry desert and scrub areas of the southwestern region of the United States, where cactus, sagebrush, and creosote bushes grow, are among the most difficult habitats in which reptiles and amphibians can live. Not many amphibians can stand the extreme heat and lack of water in a desert. Those that can survive in these conditions have developed special ways of keeping cool and moist. The red-spotted toad hides in deep crevices between rocks, while other toads escape from the heat by digging underground burrows. Here, they wait for a rainstorm which brings temporary pools where they can breed.

A desert can sometimes be too hot for reptiles, as well. Snakes and lizards need the sun's heat to give them the energy to move, but even they may hide in a burrow originally made by a small mammal to avoid the force of the midday sun. Snakes and lizards, being cold-blooded, usually sunbathe in the morning until their body reaches the correct temperature. They keep their body at the same temperature by moving in and out of the sun as needed.

Most desert animals are active at night, when the air temperature drops. A desert can become very cold at night, and keeping warm after sunset can be just as difficult for animals as keeping cool during the day.

This picture shows reptiles and amphibians—how many do you recognize?

Clockwise from top left: Gila monster (do not touch, its bite is poisonous), western whiptail, blacktail rattlesnake (avoid!), Great Plains narrowmouth toad, longnose leopard lizard, and western shovelnose snake.